SOCCER PRACTICE GAMES
FOR 6 TO 9 YEAR OLDS

by Stephen Faulkner

REEDSWAIN

**Library of Congress
Cataloging - in - Publication Data**

by Stephen Faulkner
Soccer Practice Games
for 6 to 9 Year Olds

ISBN No. 1-59164-031-8
Lib. of Congress Catalog No. 2002110533
© 2002

Editing
Bryan R. Beaver

Front Cover Photo by
Robyn McNeil

Printed by
DATA REPRODUCTIONS
Auburn, Michigan

Reedswain Publishing
612 Pughtown Road
Spring City, PA 19475
800.331.5191
www.reedswain.com
info@reedswain.com

CONTENTS

Most of the equipment used in this book is available from Reedswain. Below are just a few examples. For a free catalog of Soccer Videos, Books, Software and Equipment call us today at 800-331-5191 or visit us on the web at www.reedswain.com

Hurdle Sets

Accu-Arches

Tall Cones

Disc Cones

Small Goals

Agility Poles

HOW TO USE THIS BOOK

For Coaches of players aged 6 to 9 this book has done all of the work for you!

At the beginning of each Chapter you are told the theme of that section of the book. For example, Chapter One deals with the fundamentals of Passing, Keeping Possession and Shooting. A Coach who feels that his team needs work in any of these areas might look at the drills outlined in this Chapter.

The whole of the Chapter remains on that theme so that the Coach has a complete session planned which deals with a number of essential soccer learning experiences.

Each Chapter tells the Coach...
· The recommended playing area
· The number of players required for the drill/game
· The number of balls required for the drill or game
· How long the segment should run
· Whether bibs are required
· The number of markers needed
· Any other equipment necessary for the segment

Playing times are suggested, but each Coach will need to amend these according to the time available.

The sessions have been designed so that there is as little moving of markers and changing of the playing field aspossible. This will help to ensure that the Coaches session moves smoothly from one activity to another without the players waiting around and losing focus.

The Coach will need to gear the activities according to the abilities of his players and the coaches of the older players will find that their athletes should be able to attempt all activities in this book.

Chapter Twenty-Two provides the Coach with an effective Schedule which makes Game Day more organized and ensures a fair time for all of the players on the playing field.

All of the drills have been designed to assist the Coach in developing skilful young players who are comfortable on the ball, masters of the fundamental techniques of the game, tactically aware (even from an early age), agile, coordinated and aware of what it means to be a part of a team. At the end of most Chapters there is a time for free play with minimal coaching where the players can both implement the skills they have been taught, learn for themselves and perhaps develop new skills!

I hope you enjoy using these drills with your young players as I have with my teams in the past few years!

KIDZ ONE: A

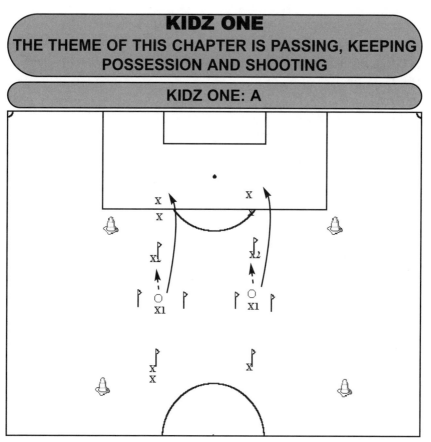

Pitch Size: 30yd x 30yd
No of players: Squad
Bibs: None
No of balls: 2 plus spares
No of markers: 4 plus 8 poles
Recommended Duration: 6 minutes

- X1 begins the drill by running with the ball towards X2
- When X1 reaches the middle markers, he passes the ball through to X2
- X1 then continues his run to join the X2 group
- X2 receives the ball and begins to run towards X3 with the ball
- When X2 reaches the markers, he passes the ball through to X3 etc, etc

- When the players become proficient at this drill, they should aim to receive, play forward and then pass to the next man. In other words they execute the drill with three touches on the ball

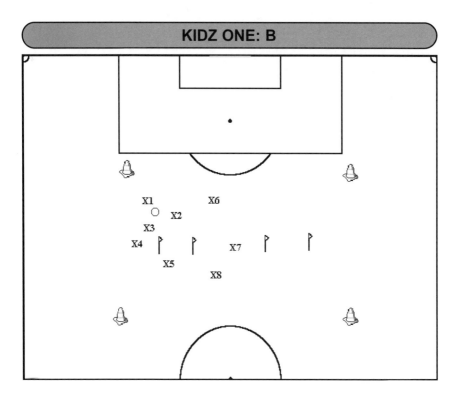

Pitch Size: 30yd x 30yd
No of players: Squad
Bibs: None
No of balls: 2 plus spares
No of markers: 4 plus 4 poles
Suggested Duration: 10 minutes

- Players play one against the rest, e.g. when the player gets the ball he has to play against everyone else in the squad
- When the player gets the ball, he tries to score through one of the two goals

- When the players become proficient at this drill or after five minutes, the coach introduces a second ball

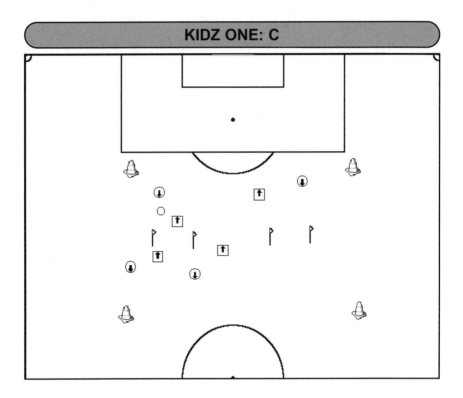

Pitch Size: 30yd x 30yd
No of players: Squad
Bibs: One or Two Sets
No of balls: 2 plus spares
No of markers: 4 plus 4 poles
Recommended Duration: 10 minutes

- Four Red players play against Four Blue players
- Each team tries to score through either goal
- Team with the most goals after 10 minutes is the winner

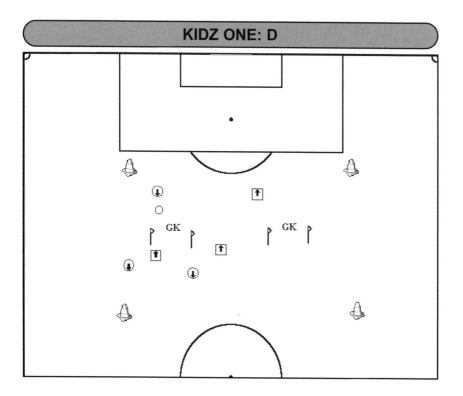

Pitch Size: 30yd x 30yd
No of players: Squad
Bibs: One or Two Sets
No of balls: 1 plus spares
No of markers: 4 plus 4 poles
Recommended Duration: 10 minutes

- Three Red players play against Three Blue players
- Each team has a goalkeeper
- Each team tries to score through their opponent's goal
- Team with the most goals after 10 minutes is the winner

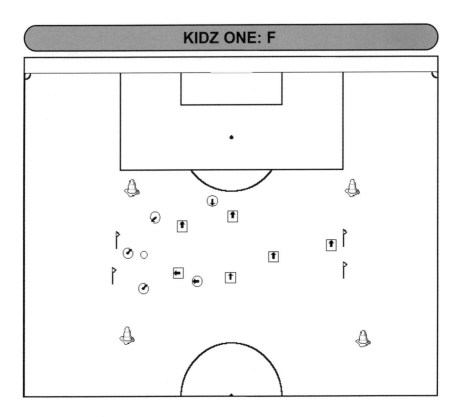

Pitch Size: 30yd x 30yd
No of players: Squad
Bibs: One or Two Sets
No of balls: 1 plus spares
No of markers: 4 plus 4 poles
Recommended Duration: 15 minutes

- Free play
- Five Reds play Five Blues in a normal game with minimal coaching, but lots of encouragement and reinforcement of good habits!

KIDZ TWO: A

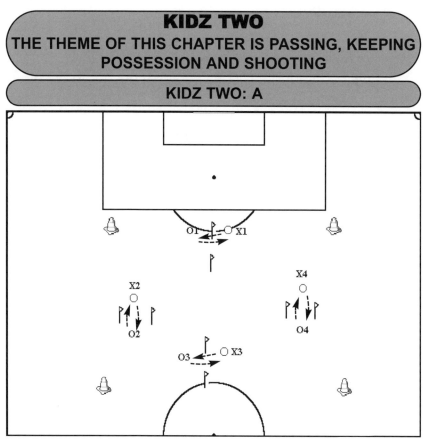

Pitch Size: 30yd x 30yd
No of players: Squad
Bibs: None
No of balls: 4 plus spares
No of markers: 4 plus 8 poles
Recommended Duration: 6 minutes

- X and O players pass the ball to each other through the markers

- At the end of one minute, all of the O players rotate onto the next X; e.g. O1 moves to X2, O2 moves to X3 etc

- X players now pick up their ball
- X1 servers a header to O1, X2 serves a header to O2 etc

- O1 heads the ball back to X1, O2 heads the ball back to X2 etc etc
- O1 now moves onto X2, O2 moves onto X3 etc etc
- X2 serves a header to O1, X3 serves a header to O2 etc etc

- After one minute O players become servers and X players head the ball

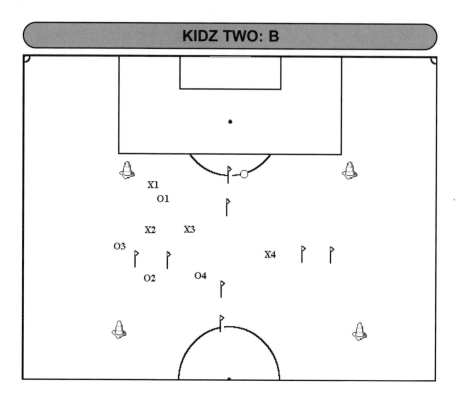

Pitch Size: 30yd x 30yd
No of players: Squad
Bibs: None
No of balls: 1 plus spares
No of markers: 4 plus 8 poles
Recommended Duration: 5 minutes

- Players play against the whole squad when they get the ball, e.g. X2 has the ball and the other seven players are his opponents
- When in possession of the ball, the players try to score through any goal

- The coach can introduce a second ball so it is easier to score goals: more goals are scored and the players get more time playing with the ball

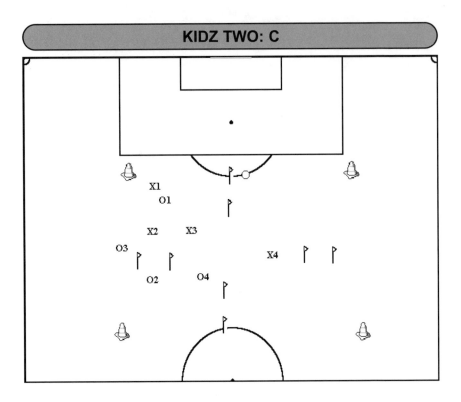

Pitch Size: 30yd x 30yd
No of players: Squad
Bibs: One or Two sets
No of balls: 1 plus spares
No of markers: 4 plus 8 poles
Recommended Duration: 10 minutes

- The players are divided into two teams
- X and O players play against each other
- When in possession of the ball, the players try to score through any goal

- The coach can introduce a second ball so it is easier to score goals, more goals are scored and the players get more time playing with the ball

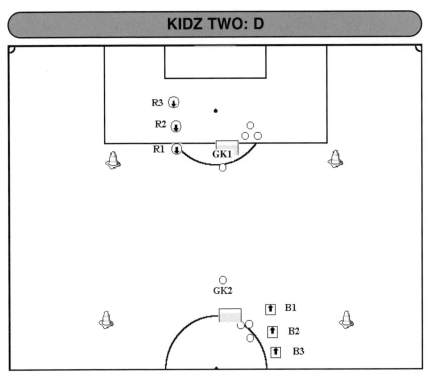

Pitch Size: 30yd x 30yd
No of players: Squad
Bibs: None
No of balls: 1 per player
No of markers: 4 plus 2 small goals
Recommended Duration: 10 minutes

- GK1 and GK2 begin the drill by throwing the ball out to R1 and B1
- R1 dribbles his ball towards GK2
- B1 dribbles his ball towards GK1
- R1 tries to score past GK2
- B1 tries to score past GK1
- R1 retrieves his ball and joins the B players
- B1 retrieves his ball and joins the R players

- GK1 and GK2 throw the ball out to R2 and B2, etc etc
- Rotate the GKs every two minutes

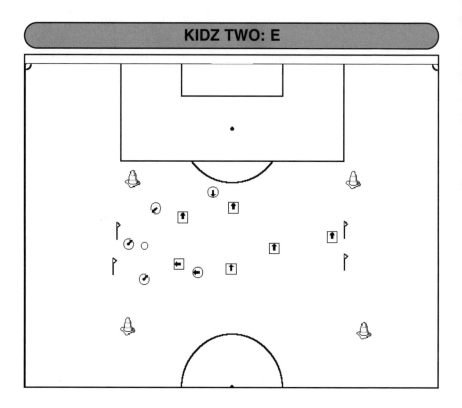

Pitch Size: 30yd x 30yd
No of players: Squad
Bibs: One or Two Sets
No of balls: 1 plus spares
No of markers: 4 plus 4 poles
Recommended Duration: 15 minutes

- Free play
- Five Reds play Five Blues in a normal game with minimal coaching, but lots of encouragement and reinforcement of good habits!

KIDZ THREE: A

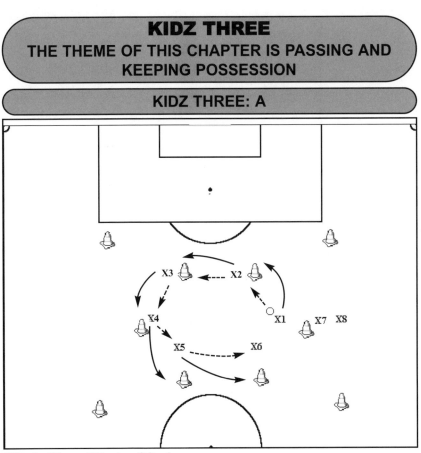

Pitch Size: 30yd x 30yd
No of players: Squad
Bibs: None
No of balls: 1 plus spares
No of markers: 10
Recommended Duration: 6 minutes

- X1 begins the drill by passing to X2
- X1 follows his pass and ends up on the X2 marker
- X2 passes the ball to X3
- X2 follows his pass and ends up on the X3 marker, etc etc

- After three minutes the players run in the opposite direction, moving around the grid in a clockwise manner

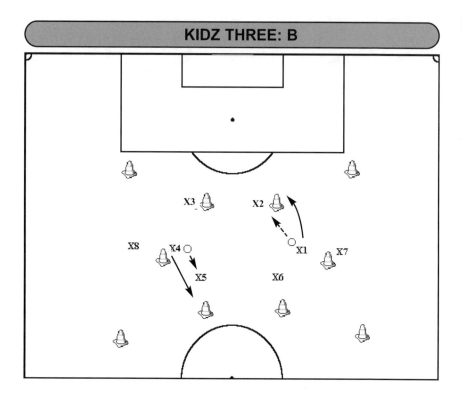

Pitch Size: 30yd x 30yd
No of players: Squad
Bibs: None
No of balls: 2 plus spares
No of markers: 10
Recommended Duration: 6 minutes

- X1 and X4 begin the drill by passing to X2 and X5
- X1 and X4 follows their pass and end up on the X2 and X5 markers
- X2 and X5 pass the ball to X3 and X6
- X2 and X5 follows their pass and end up on the X3 and X6 markers, etc etc

- After three minutes the players run in the opposite direction, moving around the grid in a clockwise manner

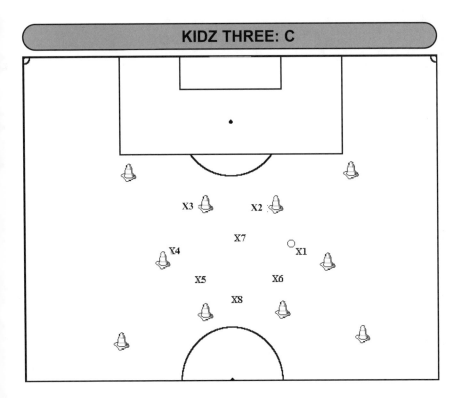

Pitch Size: 30yd x 30yd
No of players: Squad
Bibs: None
No of balls: 1 plus spares
No of markers: 10
Recommended Duration: 5 minutes

- X1 begins the drill by trying to pass the ball to any of his teammates
- The solitary defender, X7, tries to intercept X1's pass
- If X7 wins the ball, X1 becomes the defender and X7 joins the rest of the players who are trying to maintain possession
- If X7 is finding it difficult to win the ball, the coach should rotate him after a reasonable period of being the defender

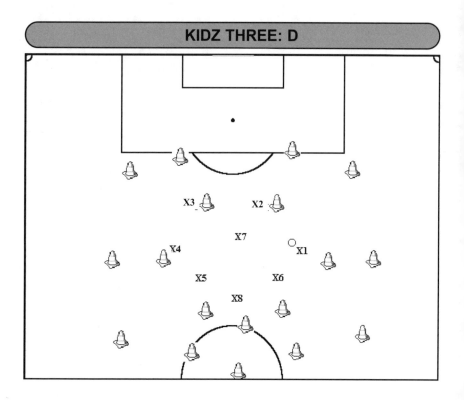

Pitch Size: 30yd x 30yd
No of players: Squad
Bibs: None
No of balls: 1 plus spares
No of markers: 18
Recommended Duration: 5 minutes

- X1 begins the drill by trying to pass the ball to any of his teammates
- If X1 makes a successful pass, he runs to the Yellow marker behind him and then back to his Red marker and back in the game
- All of the players trying to keep possession have to make the same runs (to the yellow markers and back) if they make a successful pass to one of their teammates

- The solitary defender, X7, tries to intercept X1's pass
- If X7 wins the ball, X1 becomes the defender and X7 joins the rest of the players who are trying to maintain possession
- If X7 is finding it difficult to win the ball, the coach should rotate him after a reasonable period of being the defender

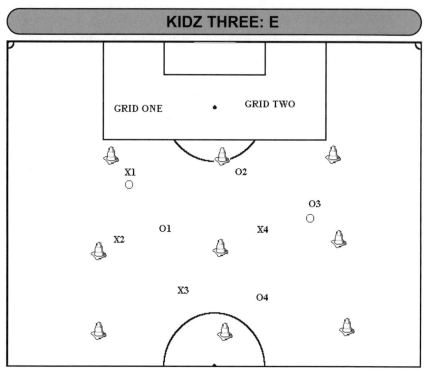

Pitch Size: 30yd x 30yd
No of players: Squad
Bibs: One or Two Sets
No of balls: 2 plus spares
No of markers: 9
Recommended Duration: 8 minutes

- X1, X2 and X3 play in grid one trying to keep the ball away from O1
- O2, O3 and O4 play in grid two trying to keep the ball away from X4

- After two minutes, rotate the defending players, e.g. X1 and O2 become defenders
- The coach should look at the movement of the X1, X2 and X3 players and the O2, O3 and O4 players and ensure that their movements create good passing angles for their team-mates

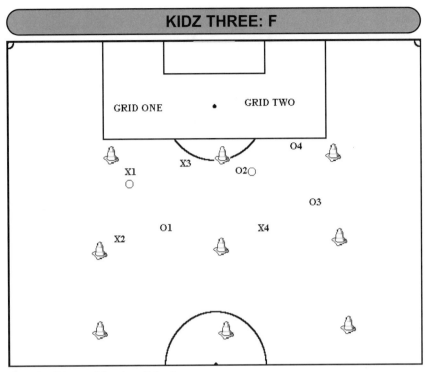

Pitch Size: 30yd x 30yd
No of players: Squad
Bibs: One or Two Sets
No of balls: 2 plus spares
No of markers: 9
Recommended Duration: 8 minutes

- X1, X2 and X3 now play in the smaller grid (15yd x 15yd) trying to keep the ball away from O1
- O2, O3 and O4 also play in the smaller grid (15yd x 15yd) trying to keep the ball away from X4
- After two minutes, rotate the defending players, e.g. X1 and O2 become defenders
- The coach should look at the movement of the players and ensure that their movements create good passing angles for their teammates
- This becomes even more important now that the area is smaller and the players in possession have less time on the ball

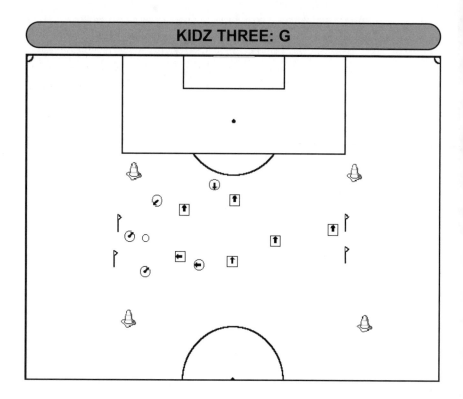

Pitch Size: 30yd x 30yd
No of players: Squad
Bibs: One or Two Sets
No of balls: 1 plus spares
No of markers: 4 plus 4 poles
Recommended Duration: 15 minutes

- Free play
- Five Reds play Five Blues in a normal game with minimal coaching, but lots of encouragement and reinforcement of good habits!

KIDZ FOUR: A

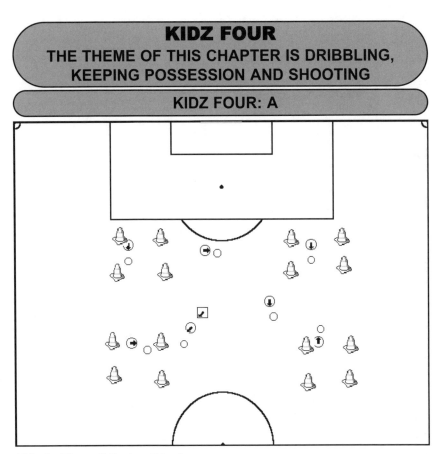

Pitch Size: 30yd x 30yd
No of players: Squad
Bibs: None
No of Balls: 1 per player
No of Markers: 16
Recommended Duration: 5 minutes

- The 7 Red players have a ball each
- The solitary Blue player is a "Tagger"
- The tagger tries to tag one of the Reds so that they become the tagger and the Blue becomes one of the players with a ball
- The Reds are safe from the tagger in the four corner squares
- Only 1 Red player is allowed in each corner

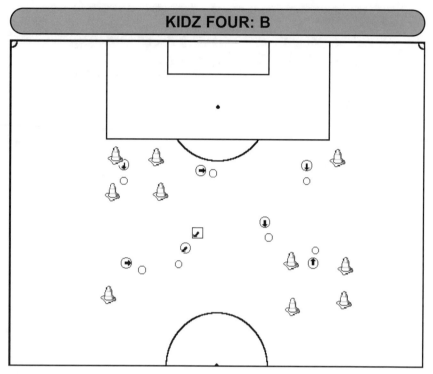

Pitch Size: 30yd x 30yd
No of players: Squad
Bibs: None
No of Balls: 1 per player
No of Markers: 10
Recommended Duration: 5 minutes

- The 7 Red players have a ball each
- The solitary Blue player is a "Tagger"
- The tagger tries to tag one of the Reds so that they become the tagger and the Blue become one of the players with a ball
- The Reds are safe from the tagger in the two corner squares
- Only 1 Red player is allowed in each corner
- Now that there are only two corner squares for the Reds means that the taggers job becomes easier and the players on the ball have to work harder to avoid being tagged

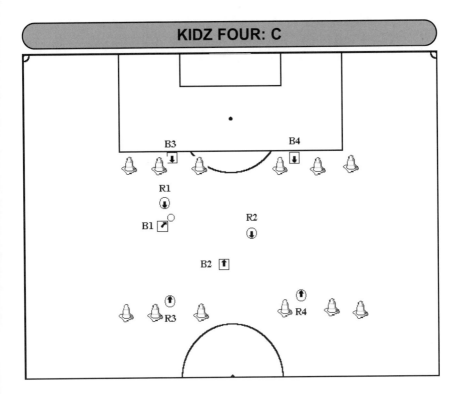

Pitch Size: 30yd x 30yd
No of players: Squad
Bibs: None
No of Balls: 1 plus spares
No of Markers: 12
Recommended Duration: 5 minutes

- B1 and B2 play against R1 and R2 in the square
- B1 and B2 try to pass the ball to B3 or B4
- If they successfully make such a pass, they swap roles.
For example, if B1 passes the ball to B3, B3 joins B2 in the
game and B1 takes B3's spot in the small goal

- R1 and R2 try to win the ball so that they can pass to R3
and R4 and swap roles

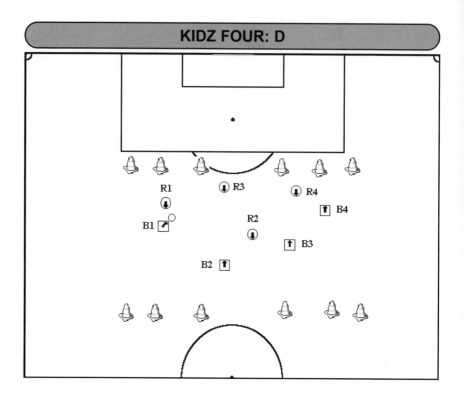

Pitch Size: 30yd x 30yd
No of players: Squad
Bibs: None
No of Balls: 1 plus spares
No of Markers: 12
Recommended Duration: 10 minutes

- All Blue players play against all of the Red players in the square
- Each team has two goals to attack

- The coach should encourage the players to switch the ball accross the pitch and attack both goals

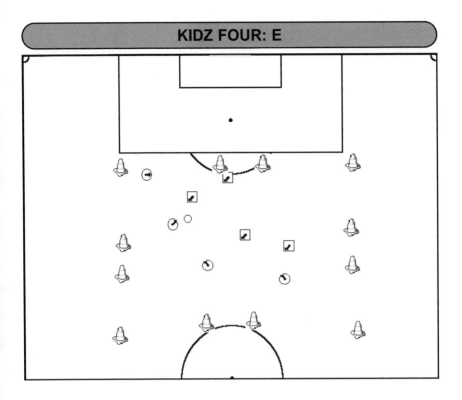

Pitch Size: 30yd x 30yd
No of players: Squad
Bibs: One or Two Sets
No of markers: 12
Balls: 1 plus spares
Recommended Duration: 10 minutes

- 4 Blue players play against 4 Red players
- Each team tries to score in two of the goals, e.g. the Blues score through the Red markers, and the Reds score through the Blue markers.

KIDZ FOUR: F

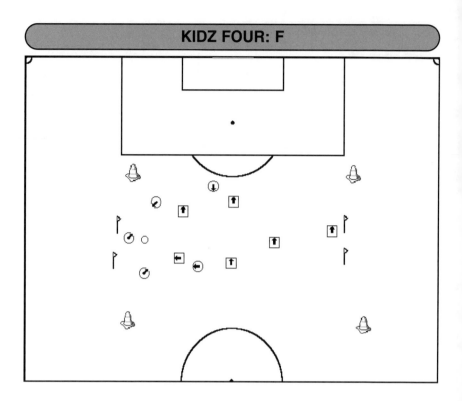

Pitch Size: 30yd x 30yd
No of players: Squad
Bibs: One or Two Sets
No of balls: 1 plus spares
No of markers: 4 plus 4 poles
Recommended Duration: 15 minutes

- Free play
- Five Reds play Five Blues in a normal game with minimal coaching, but lots of encouragement and reinforcement of good habits!

KIDZ FIVE

THE THEME OF THIS CHAPTER IS TURNING, RUNNING WITH THE BALL, TURNING AND PASSING, CREATING THROUGH BALLS AND SHOOTING

KIDZ FIVE: A

Pitch Size: 30yd x 30yd
No of players: Squad
Bibs: None
No of balls: 1 per player
No of markers: 14
Recommended Duration: 6 minutes

- Players have their own space to work in between two markers 3 yards apart
- Players run with the ball on their right foot to the marker in front of them
- At the marker, the players roll the ball behind them with the sole of their right foot

- Players then turn and run back to their original marker with the ball on their right foot
- At that marker they roll the ball behind them with the sole of their right foot
- Continue this drill for one minute

- After one minute the players perform the same drill, but with their left foot

- Players now run with the ball on their right foot
- When they reach the marker in front of them, they turn with the instep of their right foot
- Continue this drill for two minutes

- Perform the same drill as above but with the players using their left foot

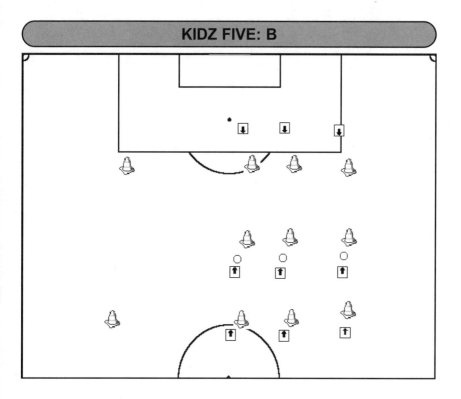

Pitch Size: 30yd x30yd
No of players: Squad
Bibs: None
No of balls: 1 per group of 3 players
No of markers: 14
Recommended Duration: 3 minutes

- The first players in the three groups jog out with the ball to the central markers
- At the markers they change their pace and accelerate to their team mate in front of them
- They pass the ball to that team mate
- The next player now jogs with a ball to the central markers
- At the markers they change their pace and accelerate to their team mate in front of them, etc etc

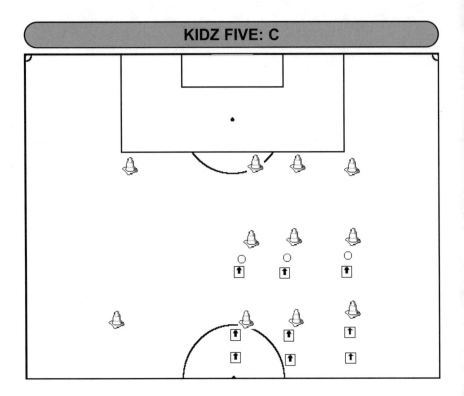

Pitch Size: 30yd x30yd
No of players: Squad
Bibs: None
No of balls: 1 per group of 3 players
No of markers: 14
Recommended Duration: 2 minutes

- The first players in the three groups jog out with the ball to the central markers
- At the markers they turn to face their group
- Players then accelerate towards their teammates
- They pass the ball to the next player in line
- The next player now jogs with ball to the central markers
- At the markers they turn and accelerate to the next man in line, etc etc

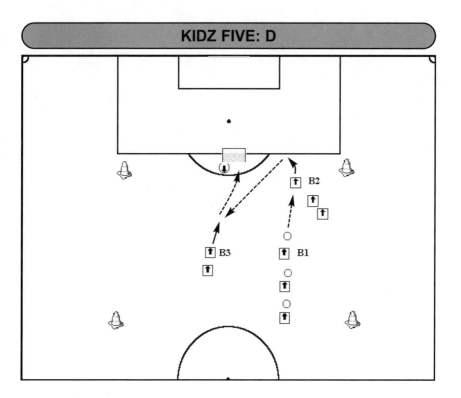

Pitch Size: 30yd x 30yd
No of players: Squad
Bibs: None
No of balls: 1 for every three players
No of markers: 4
No of Goals: 1 small goal
Recommended Duration: 10 minutes

- B1 begins the drill by passing the ball to B2
- B2 dribbles the ball forwards
- When B2 reaches the goal line, he turns and passes the ball into the path of the running B3
- B3 shoots at goal

- Players rotate, B1- B2; B2 - B3; B3 - B1

- Rotate the goalkeeper every 10 - 20 shots

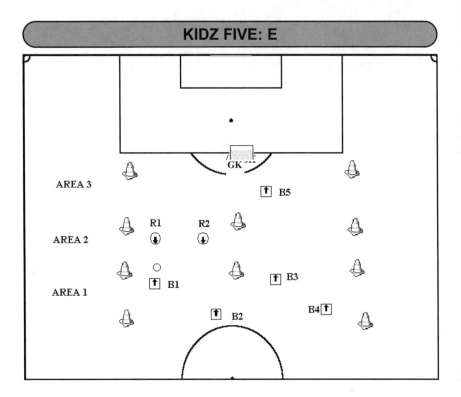

Pitch Size: 30yd x 30yd
No of players: Squad
Bibs: One or Two sets
No of balls: 1 plus spares
No of markers: 10
No of Goals: 1 small goal
Recommended Duration: 15 minutes

- B1, B2, B3 and B4 play in Area 1 only
- R1 and R2 play in Area 2 only
- B5 and the GK play in Area 3 only

- B1, B2, B3 and B4 pass the ball between them in their area

34

- Whenever they can they pass the ball through Area 2 to B5 so that B5 can shoot at the goal
- B5 must move to get open to receive the ball, he cannot go to sleep when the ball is being passed amongst his teammates!

- R1 and R2 try to get in the way and block the through pass

- B1, B2, B3 and B4 must be patient and move the two defenders around their area to eventually make a gap for the ball to be played through to B5
- B5 must move to create a passing angle

- The Coach should rotate the players and their roles

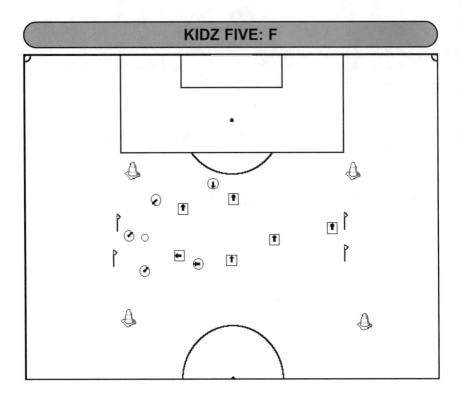

Pitch Size: 30yd x 30yd
No of players; Squad
Bibs: One or Two Sets
No of balls: 1 plus spares
No of markers: 8
Recommended Duration; 15 minutes

- Free play
- Five Reds play Five Blues in a normal game with minimal coaching, but lots of encouragement and reinforcement of good habits!

KIDZ SIX: A

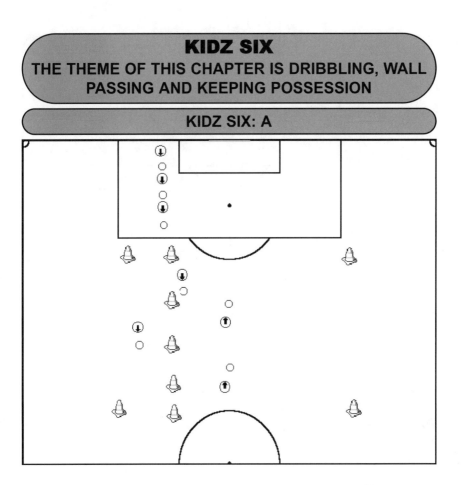

Pitch Size: 30yd x 30yd
No of players: Squad
Balls: 1 per player
Bibs: None
Markers: 4 + 5 or 6
Recommended Duration: 3 minutes

- Players dribble through the markers to the top of the grid
- Once they reach the top, the players jog back to where they came from with the ball

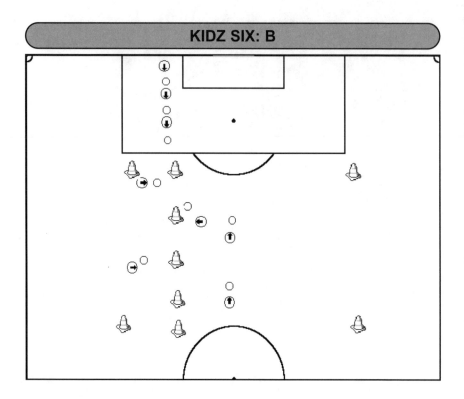

Pitch Size: 30yd x 30yd
No of players: Squad
Balls: 1 per player
Bibs: None
Markers: 4 + 5 or 6
Recommended Duration: 3 minutes

- Players dribble through the markers to the top of the grid
- Unlike the previous drill, the players do not run in a North to South fashion; instead they still travel from North to South, but by running West to East, East to West, etc as in the diagram above
- Once they reach the top, the players jog back to where they came from with the ball

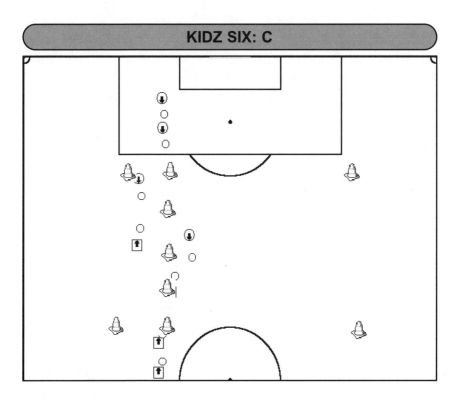

Pitch Size: 30yd x 30yd
No of players: Squad
Balls: 1 per player
Bibs: None
Markers: 4 + 5 or 6
Recommended Duration: 3 minutes

- The coach starts some of the players at the top of the markers and some at the bottom
- On the coaches signal the first two players in each group begin to dribble through the markers
- The next two quickly follow, and the next etc
- The players now have to negotiate both the markers and other players coming in the opposite direction
- The coach must instruct the players to try to run with their heads up so that they can see what they have to dribble around

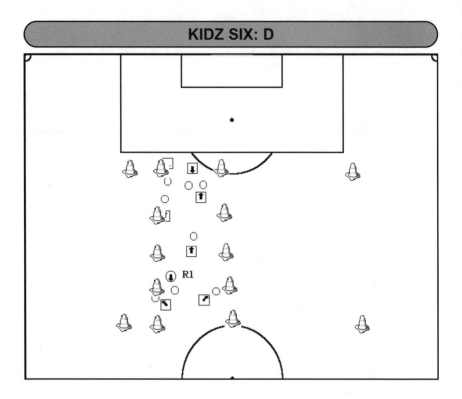

Pitch Size: 30yd x 30yd
No of players: Squad
Balls: 1 per player
Bibs: One for the defender
Markers: 4 + 10 or 12
Recommended Duration: 6 minutes

- The coach sets out a narrow channel, 1- 2yd wide and the length of the grid
- One player is picked to be the tag man (R1)
- All of the other players must dribble up and down the grid with their ball trying to avoid R1's tag
- When R1 approaches them, the Blue players may dribble the ball out of the grid to avoid the tag. R1 must stay in the channel.
- R1 becomes a Blue if he can tag. Alternatively the coach may give each player the chance to be a tag man

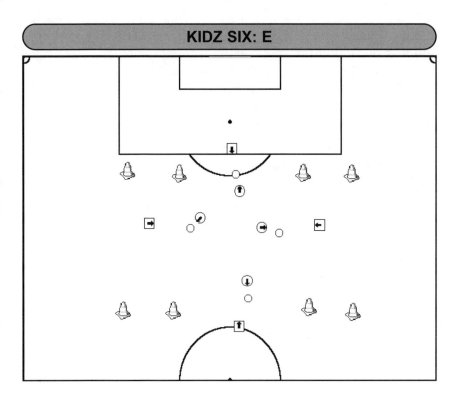

Pitch Size: 30yd x 30yd
No of players: Squad
Balls: 1 per player
Bibs: One or two sets
Markers: 8
Recommended Duration: 12 minutes

- The coach sets out a wider channel than the previous grid, 20yd x 30yd
- Outside the grid or channel are 4 wall passing players
- Inside the grid are the workers
- The workers move around the grid counter-clockwise, playing wall passes with the outside players
- After two minutes the workers and wall passers change roles

- After a further two minutes the players swap roles again, but this time they run clockwise
- After two minutes the players swap roles once more

- The players change roles again
- The Coach must now insist that the players do not monotonously move around in a circle playing each wall passer in turn, but that they turn and make unpredictable runs before playing their wall pass
- After two minutes, rotate the players

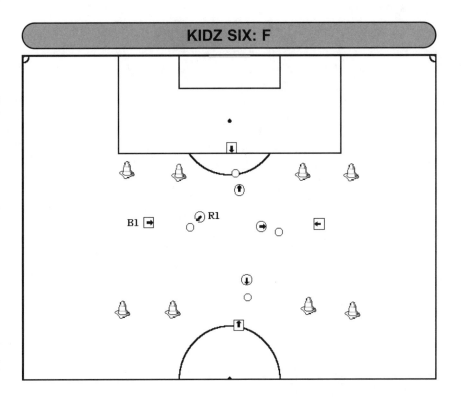

Pitch Size: 30yd x 30yd
No of players: Squad
Balls: 1 per player
Bibs: One or two sets
Markers: 8
Recommended Duration: 4 minutes

- The coach uses the same sized grid as in the last drill
- Players inside the grid (i.e. R1) look to pass to players outside the grid (i.e. B1)
- Once the pass has been made the players immediately swap roles
- R1 therefore takes B1's position and B1 runs into the grid with the ball
- B1 now looks to pass to an outside player so that they can interchange
- Continue this fast moving interchange drill for 4 minutes

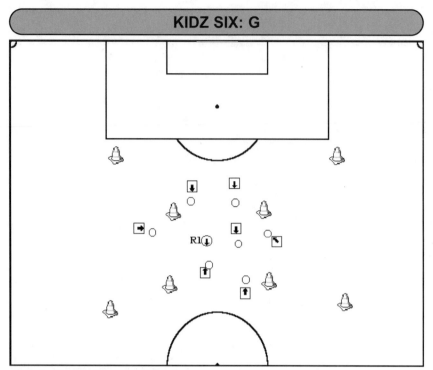

Pitch Size: 30yd x 30yd
No of players: Squad
Balls: 1 per player except for the defender
Bibs: One for the the defender
Markers: 8
Recommended Duration: 6 minutes

- The coach sets out a smaller grid than in the last drill
- One defender without a ball is placed in the middle of the grid (R1)
- All other players have a ball
- The aim of the players with the ball is to run through the grid without being tackled and without losing possession of their ball. Each time they do this they score a point
- R1 aims to win a ball and in doing so pass on his defending duties to the player tackled
- If R1 finds it hard to win a tackle, the coach rotates him with a teammate

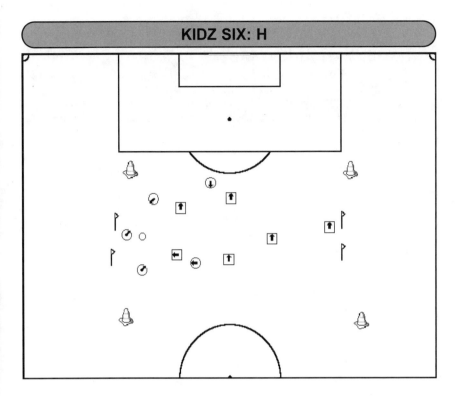

Pitch Size: 30yd x 30yd
No of players: Squad
Bibs: One or Two Sets
No of balls: 1 plus spares
No of markers: 8
Recommended Duration: 15 minutes

- Free play
- Five Reds play Five Blues in a normal game with minimal coaching, but lots of encouragement and reinforcement of good habits!

KIDZ SEVEN: A

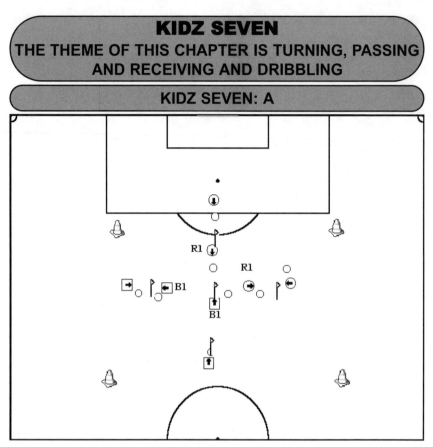

Pitch Size: 30yd x 30yd
No of players: Squad
Balls: 1 per player
Bibs: None
No of markers: 4 plus 5 poles
Recommended Duration: 3 minutes

- B1 and R1 dribble to the middle pole with the ball
- When they get to the middle, they turn on the inside of their right foot and head to the poles to their left
- Their teammates do likewise
- When all of their teammates have completed the run, B1 and R1 dribble to the middle pole again
- Once there, they turn on the inside of their left foot and return to the original pole and their teammates do likewise

46

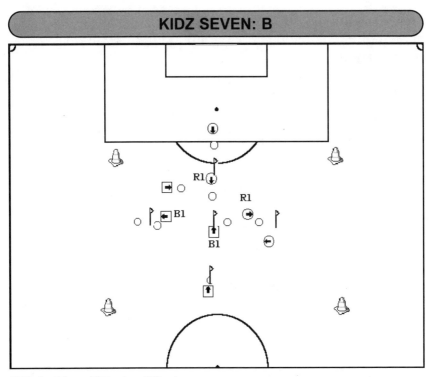

Pitch Size: 30yd x 30yd
No of players: Squad
Balls: 1 per player
Bibs: None
Markers: 4 plus 5 poles
Recommended Duration: 12 minutes

- B1 and R1 dribble to the middle pole with the ball as in the previous drill
- When they get to the middle, they turn on the inside of their right foot and head to the poles to their left
- Their teammates do likewise
- This time when B1 and R1 reach the second pole, they immediately turn and head for the middle pole again
- Unlike the previous drill where the players had a rest, this time they are moving all of the time

- Once at the middle marker they turn on the inside of their right foot and continue moving around the grid in a clock-wise manner

- After three minutes the coach reverses the players runs and makes them move anti - clockwise
- Now the players will have to turn on the inside of their left foot

- After three minutes the players are instructed to run clock-wise again
- When they get to the middle flag/marker they now turn with the outside of their left foot

- After three more minutes the players dribble in a counter - clockwise fashion
- They now use the outside of their right foot

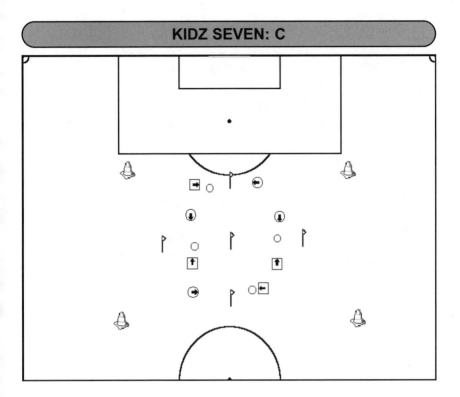

Pitch Size: 30yd x 30yd
No of players: Squad
Balls: 1 per pair
Bibs: One or two sets
Markers: 4 plus 5 poles
Recommended Duration: 8 minutes

- The players now pair off
- For one minute they pass the ball back and forth to each other with the inside of their right foot
- They then change and use their left foot for one minute

- Red players now remain in their positions
- Blue players move around the grid for one minute passing the ball to the Red servers in sequence e.g. B1 passes the ball to R1. B1 moves on to R2. B1 receives a pass from R2. B1 passes the ball to R2. B1 moves on to R3 etc etc

- Change the players roles after one minute

- The Red players become servers again
- This time they pick their balls up
- The Reds serve the Blues with a header
- The Blues move around the grid from server to server systematically
- Rotate after one minute

- The Red players become servers again and pick the balls up
- This time the ball is played to the Blue players chest
- Blue players control the ball and then return it to the Red server
- Rotate after one minute

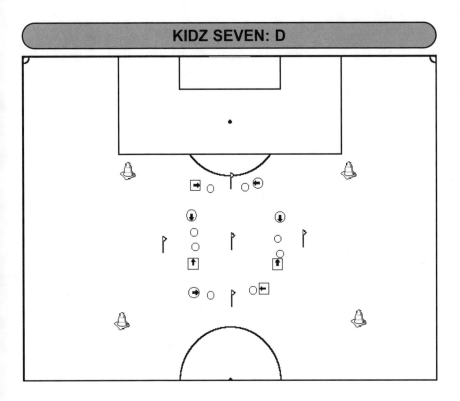

Pitch Size: 30yd x 30yd
No of players: Squad
Balls: 1 per player
Bibs: One or two sets
Markers: 4 plus 5 poles
Recommended Duration: 6 minutes

- The players once more pair off
- This time they each have a ball
- On the coaches call, they run directly at their partners with the ball
- Just before they collide, the players dribble the ball to the right
- They then run 3 yards, turn and perform the same movement again

- After three minutes they dribble to the left

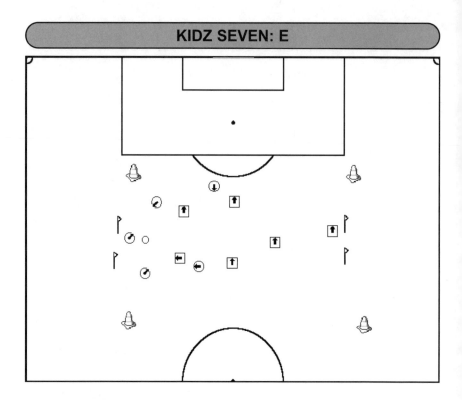

Pitch Size: 30yd x 30yd
No of players: Squad
Bibs: One or Two Sets
No of balls: 1 plus spares
No of markers: 4 plus 4 poles
Recommended Duration: 15 minutes

- Free play
- Five Reds play Five Blues in a normal game with minimal coaching, but lots of encouragement and reinforcement of good habits!

KIDZ EIGHT: A

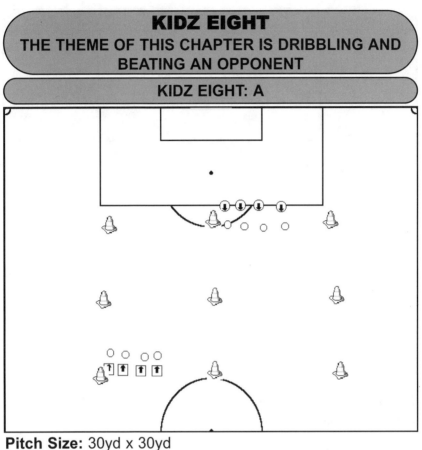

Pitch Size: 30yd x 30yd
No of players: Squad
Bibs: One or Two Sets
No of balls: 1 per player
No of markers: 9
Recommended Duration: 5 minutes

- Blue and Red players run the ball to the first line of markers
- At that line they turn and dribble back to where they came from
- Continue for two and a half minutes
- Players then run to the top of the grid, turn and dribble back to the start
- Continue for two and a half minutes

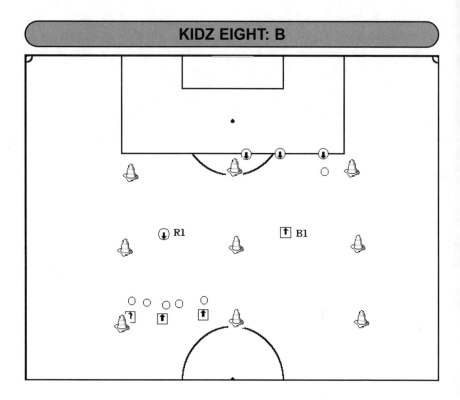

Pitch Size: 30yd x 30yd
No of players: Squad
Bibs: One or Two Sets
No of balls: 1 per attacking player
No of markers: 9
Recommended Duration: 4 minutes

- Blue and Red players attempt to dribble with the ball from the bottom of their grid to the top
- The defenders on the line (B1 and R1) attempt to stop them
- B1 and R1 can only work along the line between the two markers

- Swap the defender every minute

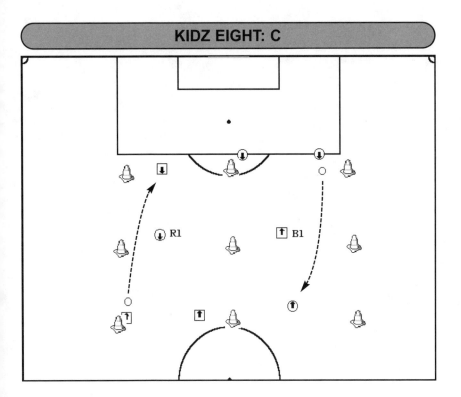

Pitch Size: 30yd x 30yd
No of players: Squad
Bibs: One or Two Sets
No of balls: 1 per three attacking players
No of markers: 9
Recommended Duration: 4 minutes

- Blue and Red players attempt to pass the ball to each other
- The defenders on the line (B1 and R1) attempt to intercept the ball as it passes from one side of the grid to the other
- B1 and R1 can only work along the line between the two markers

- Swap the defender every minute

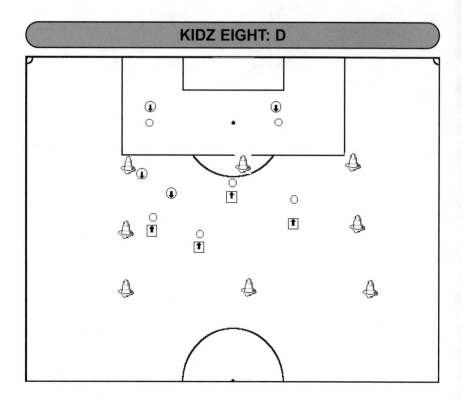

Pitch Size: 30yd x 30yd
No of players: Squad
Bibs: One or Two Sets
No of balls: 1 per attacking players
No of markers: 8
Recommended Duration: 6 minutes

- Coach asks two of the Red team to sit out
- While sitting out, the two Reds juggle their ball
- The other two Red's are defenders who attempt to stop the Blues crossing the line behind them
- As suggested, the Blue players must try to dribble past the Red players and cross the line
- Succesful Blues jog back to the starting point and try to dribble over the line again
- Reds do not tackle them when they jog back

- The Coach should encourage the defenders to "double team", so that both defenders try to stop one attacking player before moving onto the next one

- After the Red's have stopped the last Blue, the other two Reds become the defender and the drill is repeated

- If the attacking team is too good, the coach changes the defenders after a reasonable time

- Once both sets of Reds have defended, the players swap roles and the Blues become the defenders and the Reds become the attackers

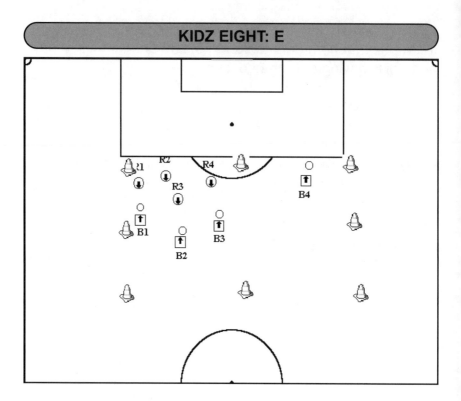

Pitch Size: 30yd x 30yd
No of players: Squad
Bibs: One or Two Sets
No of balls: 1 per attacking players
No of markers: 8
Recommended Duration: 6 minutes

- The Red team are defenders who attempt to stop the Blues crossing the line behind them
- As suggested, the Blue players must try to dribble past the Red players and cross the line
- Succesful Blues jog back to the starting point and try to dribble over the line again
- Reds do not tackle them when they jog back

- The Coach should encourage the defenders to act like a wolf pack and be prepared to let players like B4 escape so that they can "gang up" on B1, B2 or B3. This type of marking will be very beneficial to the players when they grow older and need to learn how to defend a zone as a group

- After the Red's have stopped the last Blue, the teams swap roles

- If the attacking team is too good, the coach changes the defenders after a reasonable time

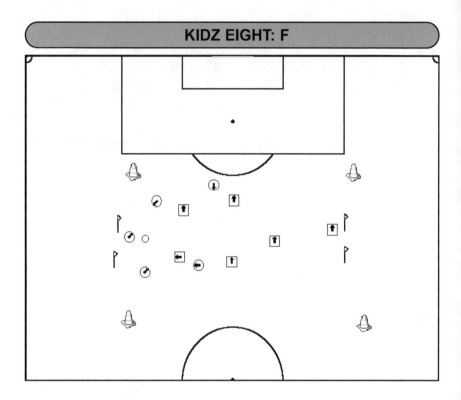

Pitch Size: 30yd x 30yd
No of players: Squad
Bibs: One or Two Sets
No of balls: 1 plus spares
No of markers: 4 plus 4 poles
Recommended Duration: 15 minutes

- Free play
- Five Reds play Five Blues in a normal game with minimal coaching, but lots of encouragement and reinforcement of good habits!

KIDZ NINE: A

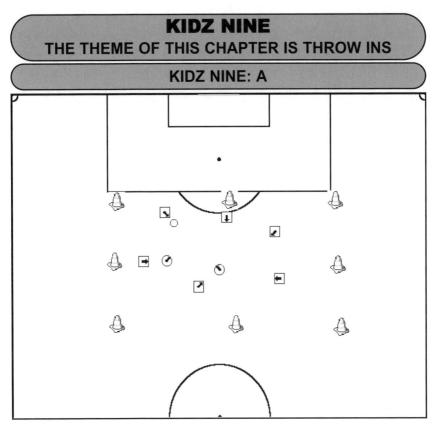

Pitch Size: 30yd x 30yd
No of players: Squad
Bibs: One or Two Sets
No of balls: 1 plus spares
No of markers: 8
Recommended Duration: 4 minutes

- 6 Blue players are faced by 2 Red players
- The Blues must keep possession by throwing the ball in to each other

- The Coach must insist on the correct throw in technique: body facing the way the ball is thrown, feet touching the ground, ball thrown from over the head, etc
- After one minute the two defenders are rotated

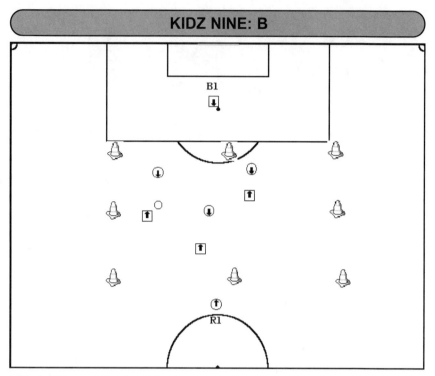

Pitch Size: 30yd x 30yd
No of players: Squad
Bibs: One or Two Sets
No of balls: 1 plus spares
No of markers: 8
Recommended Duration: 6 minutes

- 3 Blue players are faced by 3 Red players
- B1 plays with the Blues, and is the target of the Blues
- R1 plays with the Reds, and is the target of the Reds
- The teams throw the ball in to each other
- The Blues try to throw the ball to B1 and the Reds try to throw the ball to R1
- The player who makes a successful pass to B1/R1 takes his spot and the other team starts the attack
- The Coach must insist on the correct throw in technique: body facing the way the ball is thrown, feet touching the ground, ball thrown from over the head, etc

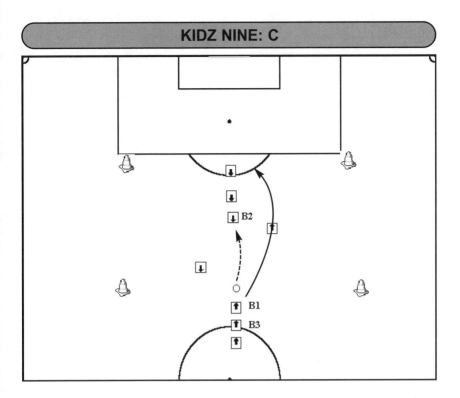

Pitch Size: 30yd x 30yd
No of players: Squad
Bibs: None
No of balls: 1 plus spares
No of markers: 4
Recommended Duration: 4 minutes

- B1 throws the ball to B2
- B1 then runs to join the B2 group
- B2 picks up the ball and throws it to B3
- B2 then runs to join the B3 group

- The Coach must insist on the correct throw in technique: body facing the way the ball is thrown, feet touching the ground, ball thrown from over the head, etc

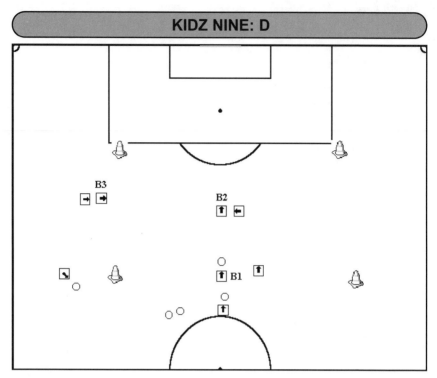

Pitch Size: 30yd x 30yd
No of players: Squad
Bibs: None
No of balls: 4 plus spares
No of markers: 4
Recommended Duration: 4 minutes

- B1 throws the ball square to B2. Many young players have problems throwing the ball square and often only look down the line to play the ball
- B1 runs to join the B2 group
- B2 then passes to B3
- B2 runs to join the B3 group
- B3 runs the ball to the B1 group
- Repeat
- The Coach must insist on the correct throw in technique: body facing the way the ball is thrown, feet touching the ground, ball thrown from over the head, etc

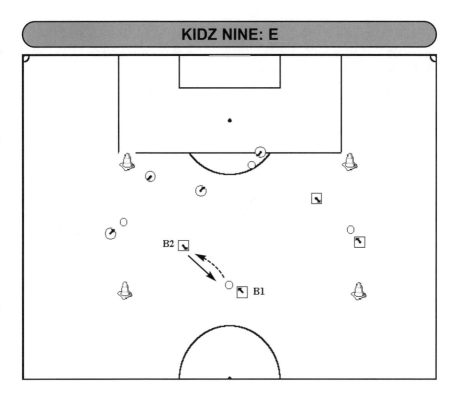

Pitch Size: 30yd x 30yd
No of players: Squad
Bibs: None
No of balls: 4 plus spares
No of markers: 4
Recommended Duration: 4 minutes

- Put the players in pairs with one ball for each pair
- B1 throws the ball down the line to his partner B2
- The Coach should ensure there is a reasonable space between B1 and B2 and that they are not too close to each other. This will make retaining possession easier

- B2, or the receiving player, passes it straight back to the thrower B1

- In the game many young players receive the ball down the line, turn and try to run towards goal and often "turn into legs" or turn into the tackle of an opponent
- By playing the ball back to the thrower the team is more likely to retain possession.

- The players repeat the drill ten times before swapping roles

- The Coach must insist on the correct throw in technique: body facing the way the ball is thrown, feet touching the ground, ball thrown from over the head, etc

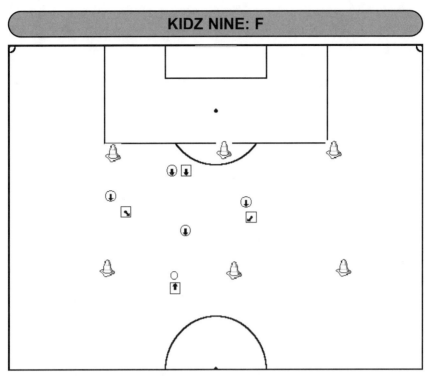

Pitch Size: 30yd x 30yd
No of players; Squad
Bibs: One or two sets
No of balls: 1 plus spares
No of markers: 6
Recommended Duration; 10 minutes

- Put the players into two teams
- The red defenders have to simply win the ball and then play it off the field for a throw in
- Each time the Reds do this they score a point
- The Blue team has to throw the ball in and try to keep the ball from being played out
- This requires the Blues to try to play effective throw ins and then keep possession once they have achieved this
- After five minutes the Blues and Reds swap roles
- As always, the Coach must insist on the correct throw in technique

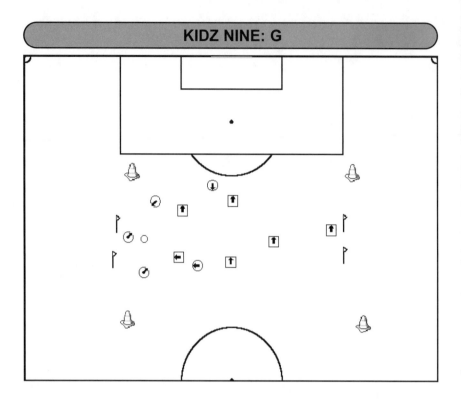

Pitch Size: 30yd x 30yd
No of players; Squad
Bibs: One or Two Sets
No of balls: 1 plus spares
No of markers: 4 plus 4 poles
Recommended Duration; 15 minutes

- Free play
- Five Reds play Five Blues in a normal game with minimal coaching, but lots of encouragement and reinforcement of good habits!

KIDZ TEN: A

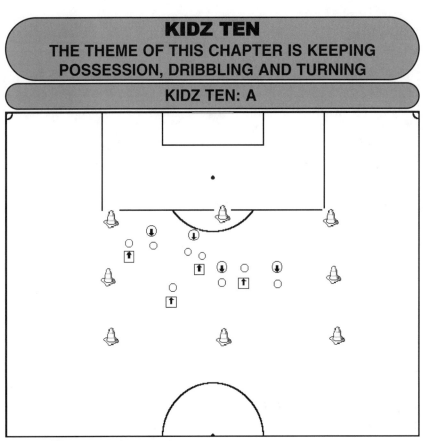

Pitch Size: 30yd x 30yd
No of players; Squad
Bibs: None
No of balls: 1 per player plus spares
No of markers: 8
Recommended Duration; 5 minutes

- Players move freely around the grid with the ball
- Players remain within the grid and therefore must turn when they come to the edges of the playing area
- Players must also ensure they do not bump into their teammates
- Coach insists and demonstrates to the players how to run with their head up (and not looking down at the ball all of the time) so that they can see what is happening around them

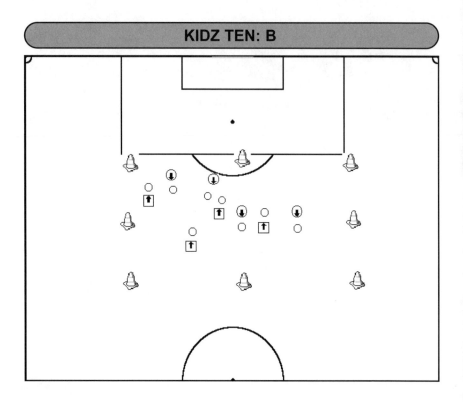

Pitch Size: 30yd x 30yd
No of players; Squad
Bibs: None
No of balls: 1 per player plus spares
No of markers: 8
Recommended Duration; 5 minutes

- Players move freely around the grid with the ball
- The Coach instructs the players to dribble around as many of his teammates as he possibly can, keeping score of each player he has "beaten" with the ball

- Players remain within the grid and therefore must turn when they come to the edges of the playing area

- Players must also ensure they do not bump into their teammates

- Coach insists and demonstrates to the players how to run with their head up (and not looking down at the ball all of the time) so that they can see

- After five minutes the Coach checks which player has dribbled the most

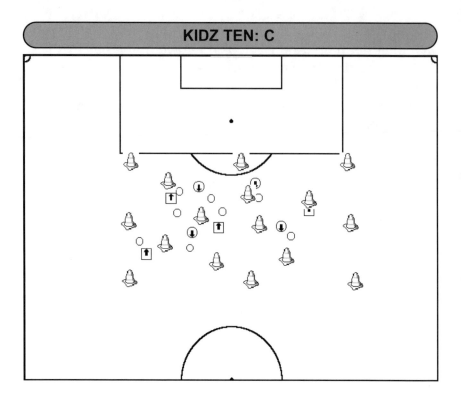

Pitch Size: 30yd x 30yd
No of players; Squad
Bibs: None
No of balls: 1 per player plus spares
No of markers: 8 + 8, 9, 10 etc
Recommended Duration; 5 minutes

- Players move freely around the grid with the ball
- The Coach places a large number of markers within the grid
- The players must dribble around as many markers as they can trying hard not to hit the ball against the markers
- The players keep score of each marker they have dribbled past without touching

- Players remain within the grid and therefore must turn when they come to the edges of the playing area

- Players must also ensure they do not bump into their teammates

- Coach insists and demonstrates to the players how to run with their head up (and not looking down at the ball all of the time) so that they can see what is happening around them

- After five minutes the Coach checks which player has dribbled the most

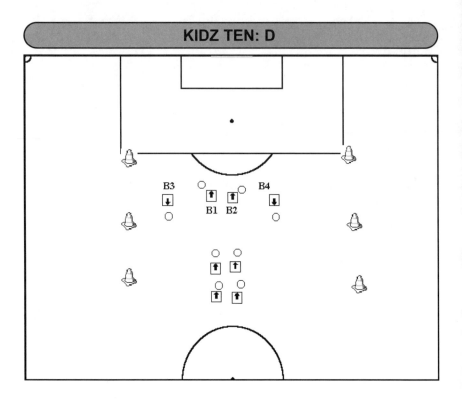

Pitch Size: 30yd x 30yd
No of players; Squad
Bibs: None
No of balls: 1 per player plus spares
No of markers: 6
Recommended Duration: 8 minutes

- Players line up as in the diagram
- B1 and B2 run to the top of the grid side by side. At the top of the grid they will turn and return to the starting point (like B3 and B4)

- The Coach allows the players to run freely for two minutes and not coach them

- After two minutes the Coach needs to pick on a player who is running with the ball near to his partner

- The Coach then makes the point that you need to run keeping the ball away from your opponent
- The Coach therefore asks the players to run like B1 and B2
- B1 runs with the ball on his left foot
- B2 runs with the ball on his right foot

- This will be a difficult drill for many one footed youngsters, but the coach should persist to turn them into both two footed and better players

- Better players will not only be able to run with the ball on the foot furthest away from their opponent, but on the outside of that foot in this instance

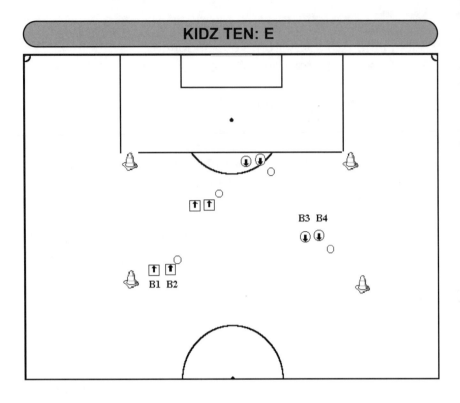

Pitch Size: 30yd x 30yd
No of players; Squad
Bibs: None
No of balls: 1 per pair plus spares
No of markers: 4
Recommended Duration; 6 minutes

- Players line up as in the diagram
- B1 and B2 run to the top of the grid side by side
- B2 has the ball on his right foot, the foot furthest away from his passive opponent
- B1 runs alongside B2 to give him the sense of opposition
- B1 does not attempt to tackle B1, merely to force him to use the correct foot to protect the ball

- At the top of the grid when B2 turns he now needs to change and use his left foot, like B4
- If he continues to use his right foot then the ball will be near his opponent
- The Coach must stop play and demonstrate this so that the players are clear as to why they need to change feet

- Better players will be able to turn comfortably at the top of the grid so that the ball is immediatly transferred from their right to left foot
- For example, the player may turn on the inside of his left foot and then play the ball with the outside of his left foot with his next touch
- Alternatively, the player may turn on the outside of his right foot and then play the ball with the outside of his left foot with his next touch

- Only the better players will be able to do this

- After three minutes the players should swap their roles

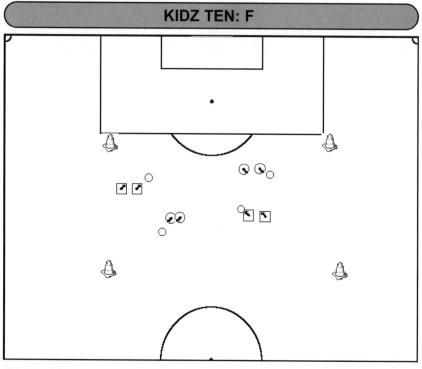

Pitch Size: 30yd x 30yd
No of players; Squad
Bibs: None
No of balls: 1 per pair plus spares
No of markers: 4
Recommended Duration; 6 minutes

- Players line up as in the diagram
- Moving freely around the grid, the player on the ball attempts to always keep the ball away from his opponent
- The opponent is no longer passive and is trying to tackle
- The opponent records each succesful tackle

- After three minutes the players should swap their roles

- At the end of the drill the players see who has been tackled the least in three minutes to see who has been the best at turning and shielding the ball

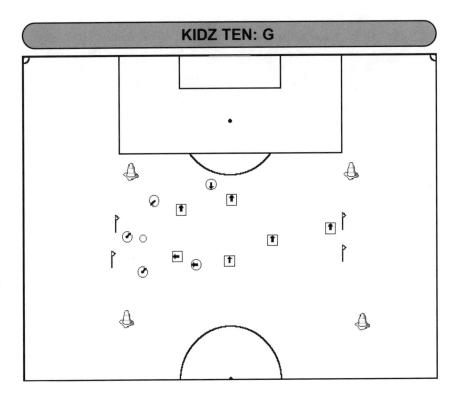

Pitch Size: 30yd x 30yd
No of players; Squad
Bibs: One or Two Sets
No of balls: 1 plus spares
No of markers: 4 plus 4 poles
Recommended Duration; 15 minutes

- Free play
- Five Reds play Five Blues in a normal game with minimal coaching, but lots of encouragement and reinforcement of good habits!

KIDZ ELEVEN: A

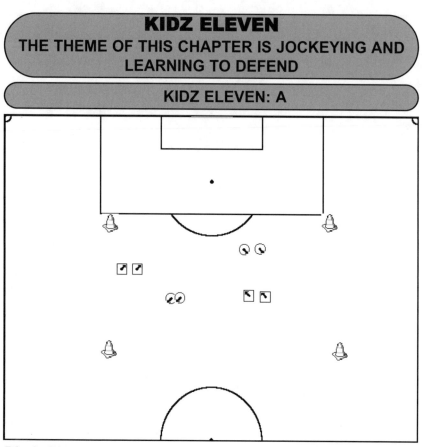

Pitch Size: 30yd x 30yd
No of players; Squad
Bibs: None
No of balls: 0
No of markers: 4
Recommended Duration: minutes

- Players line up in pairs as in the diagram
- Moving freely around the grid, the lead player moves around the square
- His partner attempts to follow him and always remain within touching distance to the lead player

- After two minutes the players swap roles

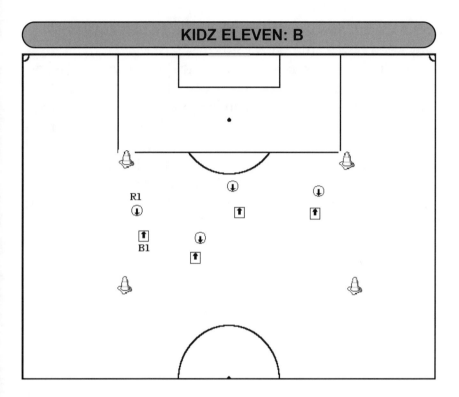

Pitch Size: 30yd x 30yd
No of players; Squad
Bibs: None
No of balls: 0
No of markers: 4
Recommended Duration; 6 minutes

- Players line up in pairs as in the diagram
- This time the lead player (R1) faces his partner
- The "defending" player (B1) attempts to stop the lead player from getting past him and always tries to be the same distance, half to one yard, from the "attacking" lead player

- The Coach needs to teach the players how to run side-ways and how to run backwards
- The Coach should always encourage the players to get side on and not get caught flat footed. It should be demon-strated to the players how standing square to the attacking player can make it easier for him to get around the defender

- The Coach may have to do this drill at walking or perhaps half pace initially so that the players can understand what is required and so that they can obtain early success in the art of jockeying

- After three minutes the players swap roles

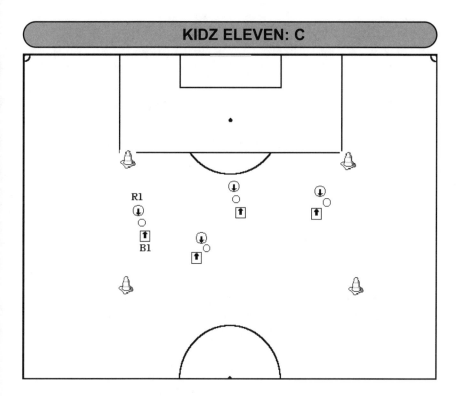

Pitch Size: 30yd x 30yd
No of players; Squad
Bibs: None
No of balls: 1 per attacking player
No of markers: 4
Recommended Duration; 6 minutes

- Players line up in pairs as in the last drill
- This time the attacking players have a ball at their feet
- Again the lead player (R1) faces his partner
- The "defending" player (B1) attempts to stop the lead player from getting past him and always tries to be the same distance, half to one yard, from the "attacking" lead player

- The Coach may have to walk players through this initially rather than expect the young players to pick up the idea immediately

- The Coach will find this difficult, but he must emphasise to the players that the object of this drill is not to tackle the attacker, but to never let him dribble past the defender.
- Many young players will not be able to help themselves and they will inevitably tackle when they see a chance to win the ball! The Coach must be very patient!

- The Coach needs to teach the players how to run sideways and how to run backwards
- The Coach should always encourage the players to get side on and not get caught flat footed. It should be demonstrated to the players how standing square to the attacking player can make it easier for him to get around the defender

- After three minutes the players swap roles

KIDZ ELEVEN: D

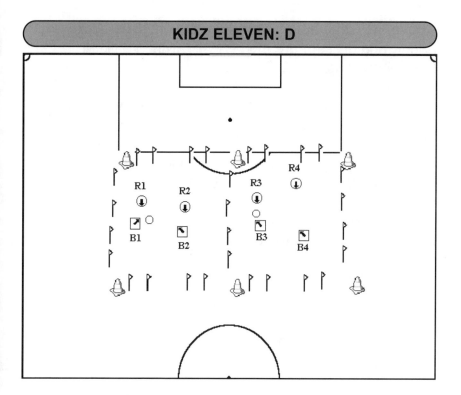

Pitch Size: 15yd x 15yd x 2
No of players; Squad
Bibs: One or two sets
No of balls: 1 per group plus spares
No of markers: 6 plus poles for goals and sideline markings
Recommended Duration; 20 minutes

- The pitch is divided into two 15yd x 15yd areas
- Each pitch has four goals
- Players are divided into four teams
- On each pitch there is a small sided game of 2 v 2, 3 v 3 etc

- The Coach allows free play to occur for five minutes
- The Coach observes the defending of the players in the game

- Have they learned anything from the previous "jockeying" or delaying drills, or are the players "diving in" like they may have done in the past?

- The Coach now has to teach the players when to jockey and when to try to win the ball

- The Coach must preach patience to the defenders, especially when the ball is a long way from the goal they are defending
- Defenders should be taught to look for when the attacker lacks good control of the ball and they may win it

- As soon as the ball is won, the Coach encourages the new attackers to score as quickly as they can

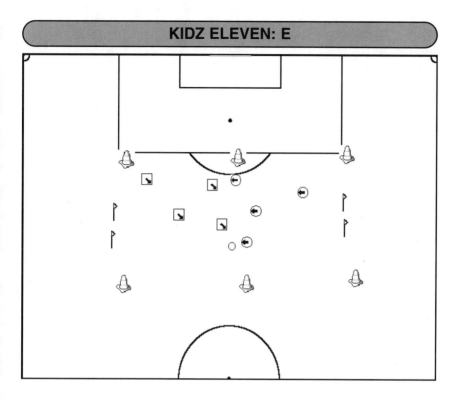

Pitch size: 30yd x 30yd
No of players: Squad
No of balls: 1 plus spares
Bibs: 1 or two sets
No of Markers: 6 plus 4 poles
Recommended duration: 25 minutes

- The players are now divided into two teams for a 4 v 4, 5 v 5 etc game

- The Coach allows the game to flow freely for five minutes
- After this time he reinforces the lessons of the previous defending drills

- If the players are quick to learn and the Coach is happy with the way they are learning to jockey and not dive in, he may introduce the players to one new point. As soon as the players are beaten by an attacker, the Coach should instruct the player to recover and get behind the ball as quicky as he can
- Many young players who find themselves beaten in a game often stay where they are rather than get back to help their teammates

- The Coach should try to end the session with 10 minutes of free play and with no demonstrations or interuptions to the play

KIDZ TWELVE
THE THEME OF THIS CHAPTER IS DRIBBLING, WALL PASSING, BEATING PLAYERS AND DIAGONAL RUNS

KIDZ TWELVE: A

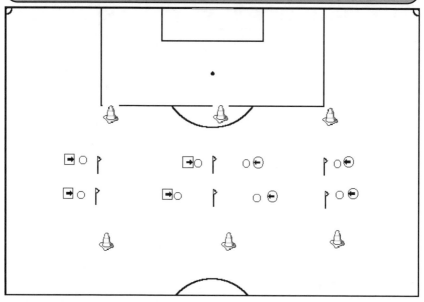

Pitch size: 30yd x 30yd
No of players: Squad
No of balls: 1 per player plus spares
Bibs: 1 or two sets
No of Markers: 6 plus 6 poles
Recommended duration: 5 minutes

- The players are divided into two groups.
- The Blues dribble the ball from their starting flag around the middle flag and then back to the start.
- They then dribble the ball to the Red group's flag at the opposite end of the grid and then return home and repeat.
- The Red players do the same
- The Coach should encourage the players to run with their heads up and make sure they do not collide with members of the other group in this warm up

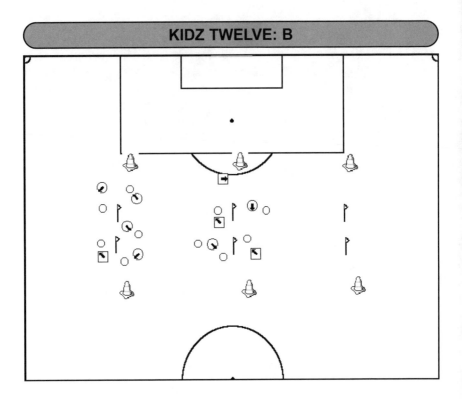

Pitch size: 30yd x 30yd
No of players: Squad
No of balls: 1 per player plus spares
Bibs: 1 or two sets
No of Markers: 6 plus 6 poles
Recommended duration: 5 minutes

- The players perform figure-eight runs through the flags

- The Coach should encourage the players to run with their heads up and make sure they do not collide with members of the other group in this warm up

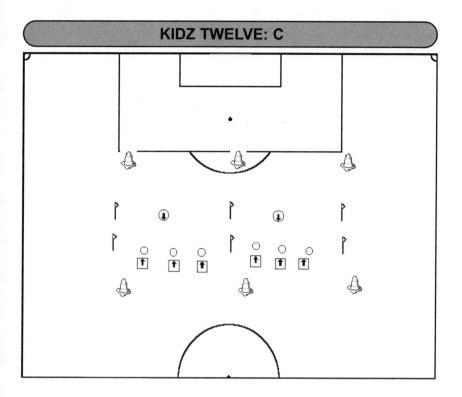

Pitch size: 30yd x 30yd
No of players: Squad
No of balls: 1 per attacking player plus spares
Bibs: 1 or two sets
No of Markers: 6 plus 6 poles
Recommended duration: 10 minutes

- The players are now divided into two teams, 3 Blues and
1 Red defender play in each half pitch
- The Red players can only stay inside the flagged area
- Red players try to stop the Blues from getting through their
zone
- If they tackle a Blue, the Blue leaves the field and juggles
his ball until the other Blues are caught

- The Blues attempt to dribble through the flagged area and reach the end zones of the grid
- They get a point for each succesful run

- Rotate the defender after he has tackled all of the attacking players, or after a reasonable time if he is finding it hard to catch all of the attackers

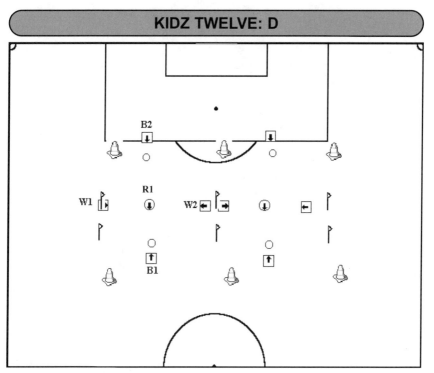

Pitch size: 30yd x 30yd
No of players: Squad
No of balls: 1 per attacking player plus spares
Bibs: 1 or two sets
No of Markers: 6 plus 6 poles
Recommended duration: 10 minutes

- B1 has the job of beating R1 and getting to the top of the grid
- B1 can beat R1 with a dribble, or with a wall pass played to either W1 to his left, or W2 to his right
- If the ball is played to W1 or W2 these wall passers must play the ball behind R1 for B1 to run onto
- Once at the top of the grid B1 rests while R1 turns around to face B2 who is also trying to get past him with a dribble or a wall pass

- Rotate the defender every one to two minutes

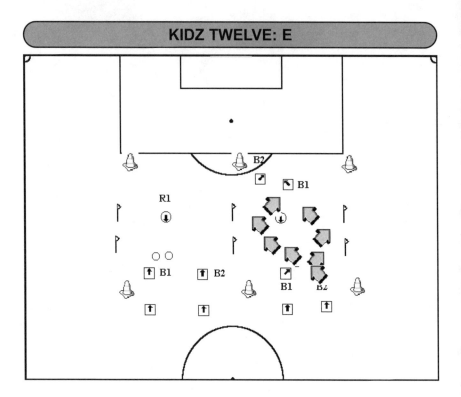

Pitch size: 30yd x 30yd
No of players: Squad
No of balls: 1 per pair of attacking players plus spares
Bibs: 1 or two sets
No of Markers: 6 plus 6 poles
Recommended duration: 15 minutes

- B1 and B2 have the job of beating R1 and getting to the top of the grid
- B1 can beat R1 with a dribble, or with a pass played to his team mate B2

- The Coach should encourage B1 and B2 to experiment and discover for themsealves how 2 can beat 1
- It is very likely amongst the younger players that B1 will try to beat R1 himself. The Coach should encourage the player to try to dribble himself, but at the same time he also needs to demonstrate how drawing R1 to B1 and then having B1 play a pass past the defender to B2 can be a very effective tool to beat defenders

- Building upon the previous drill, the Coach should encourage the players to play wall passes

- The Coach should also get the players to perform diagonal rather than straight runs (as in grid 2) in an attempt to confuse the defender
- During the diagonal runs B1 may keep the ball or he may pass it to B2 if this makes it easier to beat R1. The Coach may demonstrate to the players when it is wise to choose a particular option

- Rotate the defender every one to two minutes

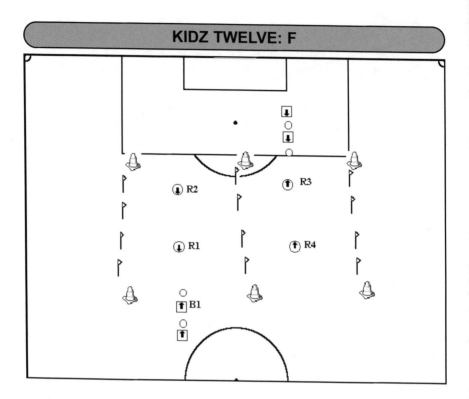

Pitch size: 30yd x 30yd
No of players: Squad
No of balls: 1 per attacking player plus spares
Bibs: 1 or two sets
No of Markers: 6 plus 12 poles
Recommended duration: 10 minutes

- The Blues have to run the Gauntlet and beat all four defenders in their defensive zones if they can
- For example, B1 has to beat R1 before moving on to R2 and then R3 etc etc
- The defenders cannot move out of their flagged zone

- If an attacker is tackled by a defender, he moves onto the next defender and tries to beat him

- Rotate the defenders every one to two minutes

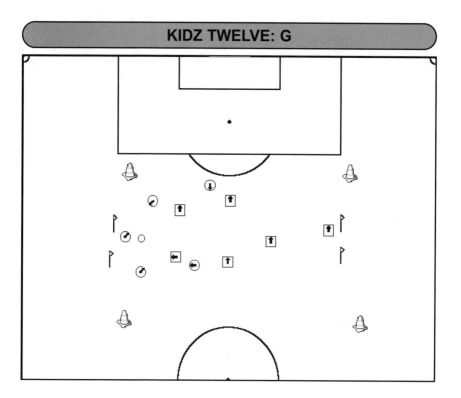

Pitch Size: 30yd x 30yd
No of players; Squad
Bibs: One or Two Sets
No of balls: 1 plus spares
No of markers: 4 plus 4 poles
Recommended Duration; 10 minutes

- Five Reds play Five Blues in a normal game, but the players must beat one of their opponents before they are allowed to pass the ball
- The players can dribble, use wall passes etc, and put into practice all of the skills they have been working on during the session

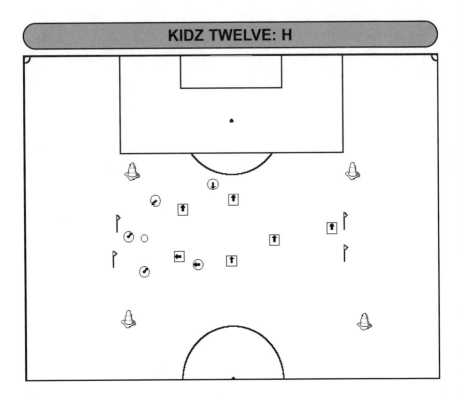

Pitch Size: 30yd x 30yd
No of players; Squad
Bibs: One or Two Sets
No of balls: 1 plus spares
No of markers: 4 plus 4 poles
Recommended Duration; 15 minutes

- Free play
- Five Reds play Five Blues in a normal game with minimal coaching, but lots of encouragement and reinforcement of good habits!

KIDZ THIRTEEN: A

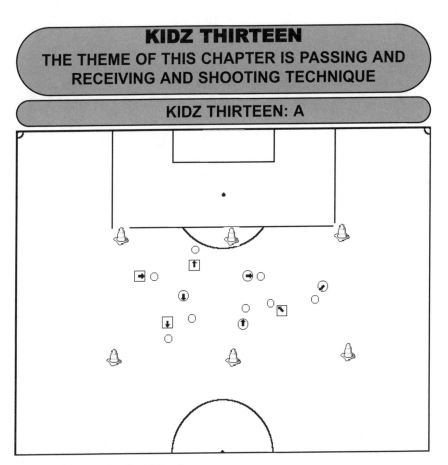

Pitch Size: 30yd x 30yd
No of players; Squad
Bibs: None
No of balls: 1 per player plus spares
No of markers: 6
Recommended Duration; 5 minutes

- The players walk around the square with their ball
- They throw the ball in the air and then head it back into their own arms
- Repeat

99

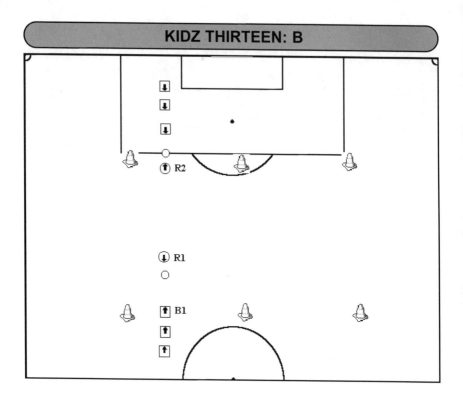

Pitch Size: 30yd x 30yd
No of players; Squad
Bibs: None
No of balls: 2 plus spares
No of markers: 6
Recommended Duration; 5 minutes

- The two servers, R1 and R2, deliver balls to the Blue players at head height
- The Blues head the balls back to the server, hopefully so that the later can catch the ball easily
- Once B1 has received a header from R1, he then runs on to the group that will get a ball from R2

- The servers are rotated every minute

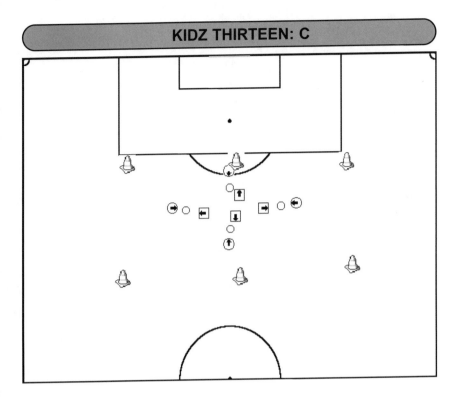

Pitch Size: 30yd x 30yd
No of players: Squad
Bibs: None
No of balls: 1 per server plus spares
No of markers: 6
Recommended Duration: 4 minutes

- The Red servers wait for a Blue player to run to them
- When the Blue player is in a position to recieve a header, the Red player plays the ball
- Blue aims to head it back into Red's arms
- Once the header has been executed, the Blue player moves on to another server

- Swap the players roles after 2 minutes

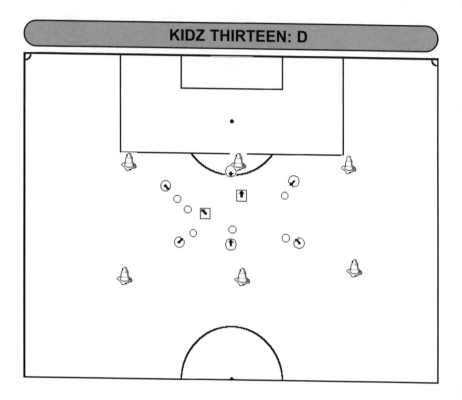

Pitch Size: 30yd x 30yd
No of players: Squad
Bibs: None
No of balls: 1 per server plus spares
No of markers: 6
Recommended Duration: 4 minutes

- The Red servers wait for a Blue player to run to them
- When the Blue player is in a position to recieve a header, the Red player plays the ball
- Blue aims to head it back into Red's arms
- Once the header has been executed, the Blue player moves on to another server

- It is likely that in the previous drill that the players would move around clockwise in a very regimented fashion from server to server

- This time the Coach insists that if they have received a header from a particular server, they now turn and seek out another server in a totally different part of the grid
- The number of servers are increased to facilitate this

- Swap the players roles after 1 minute

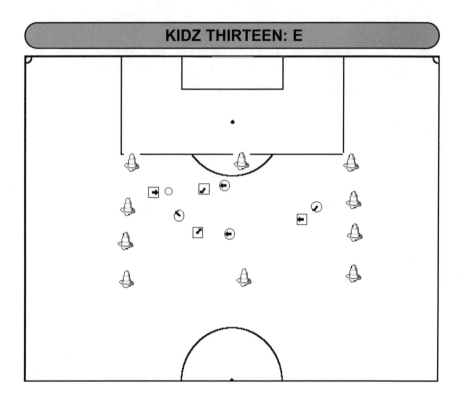

Pitch Size: 30yd x 30yd
No of players: Squad
Bibs: One or two sets
No of balls: 1 plus spares
No of markers: 10
Recommended Duration: 10 minutes

- The Reds play the Blues in a game where the object is to score headed goals
- Play starts with one player holding the ball in his hand
- He can pass the ball to his teammates basketball style

- The receiving player can catch the pass with his hands, or he can head it on to his teammates

- Goals can only be scored with a header

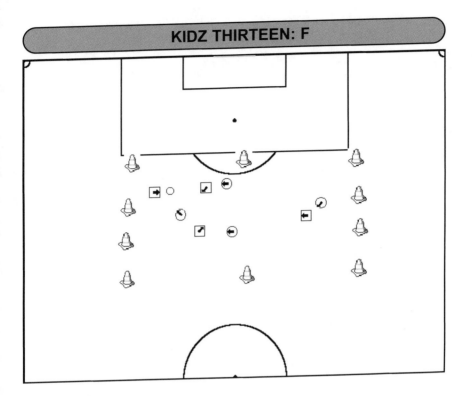

Pitch Size: 30yd x 30yd
No of players: Squad
Bibs: One or two sets
No of balls: 1 plus spares
No of markers: 10
Recommended Duration: 10 minutes

- The Reds play the Blues in a game where the object is to score headed goals
- Play starts with one player holding the ball in his hand
- He can pass the ball to his teammates basketball style

- The receiving player this time must head it on to his team-mates
- The sequence therefore becomes throw, head, catch and throw, head, catch and throw etc etc
- Goals can only be scored with a header

105

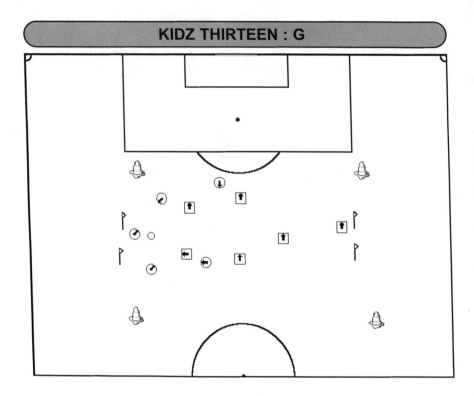

Pitch Size: 30yd x 30yd
No of players: Squad
Bibs: One or Two Sets
No of balls: 1 plus spares
No of markers: 4 plus 4 poles
Recommended Duration: 15 minutes

- Free play
- Five Reds play Five Blues in a normal game with minimal coaching, but lots of encouragement and reinforcement of good habits!

KIDZ FOURTEEN: A

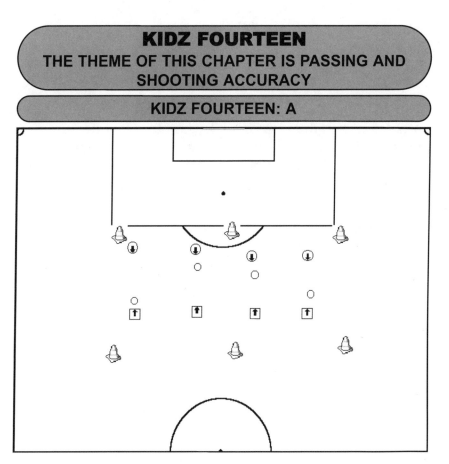

Pitch Size: 30yd x 30yd
No of players: Squad
Bibs: None
No of balls: 1 per pair of players plus spares
No of markers: 6
Recommended Duration: 4 minutes

- The players pass the ball between them
- The Coach has to insist on good technique and look for ball to be played with the side of the foot, or with the laces
- He must jump on any "toe poking" or any other poor technique

- VARIATION 1: This time the players must pass the ball with their right foot only for two minutes and then the left foot only for two minutes

- VARIATION 2: This time the players must recieve the ball on one foot and then transfer it to the other foot before passing it back to their partner. The Blue player may for example recieve the ball on his left foot and then switch it to his right foot before passing it to his Red partne

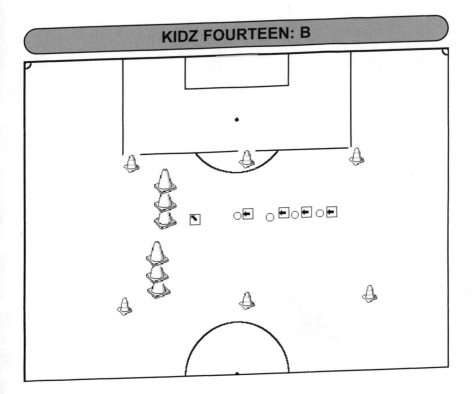

Pitch Size: 30yd x 30yd
No of players: Squad
Bibs: None
No of balls: 1 per player plus spares
No of markers: 6 plus 6 tall cones
Recommended Duration: 4 minutes

- The coach puts 6 markers out to make the basic 30 x 30 grid
- He then gets 6 tall cones and places them as in the diagram

- The players line up with the ball at their feet
- They run down the centre of the grid and shoot the ball at one of the sets of tall cones
- The cones should be so big and heavy that it is unlikely that the young soccer player will be able to knock them over

- Two small goals may serve as an alternative to the tall cones
- The Coach should encourage the players to shoot with their instep at the targets. He should stress that the players are essentially passing the ball very firmly at the goal!

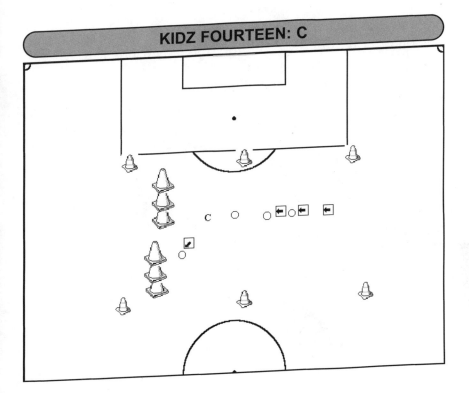

Pitch Size: 30yd x 30yd
No of players: Squad
Bibs: None
No of balls: 1 per player plus spares
No of markers: 6 plus 6 tall cones
Recommended Duration: 4 minutes

- The coach puts 6 markers out to make the basic 30 x 30 grid
- He then gets 6 tall cones and places them as in the diagram

- The players line up with the ball at their feet
- The Coach, C, stands about 10yd from the two sets of markers
- The players run down the centre of the grid towards the Coach

- When the players get close to the Coach he indicates with his left or right hand which target the player has to shoot at.

- The Coach should ensure that the players shoot at both sets of cones and that they use both feet. If the Coach knows that a particular player needs practice at using his weaker foot or shooting on his weaker side he makes sure that the player is forced to work on this weakness!

- At the same time the players want to experience success and the Coach should make sure that the excercise is not totally frustrating for the players

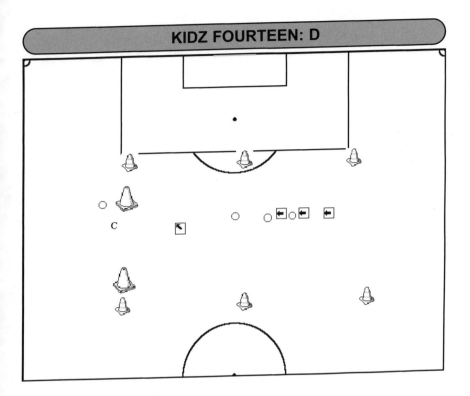

Pitch Size: 30yd x 30yd
No of players: Squad
Bibs: None
No of balls: 1 per player plus spares
No of markers: 6 plus 2 tall cones
Recommended Duration: 4 minutes

- The Coach, C, now takes two of the tall cones to make a large goal
- The Coach stays in the middle of that goal and does not move for the whole of this 4 minute drill

- The players run down the centre of the grid and have to "pass" the ball past the passive goalkeeper into the corners of the goal
- Once more the Coach should be emphasising technique and not power, or sheer "blasting" of the ball at goal

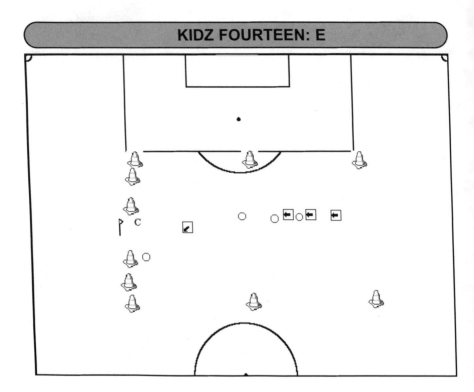

Pitch Size: 30yd x 30yd
No of players: Squad
Bibs: None
No of balls: 1 per player plus spares
No of markers: 6 plus 1 pole
Recommended Duration: 4 minutes

- The Coach, C, now makes two small goals
- The Coach (or one of the players) is the goalkeeper and this time he is able to move, but he must begin each time from the flag between the two goals
- The player can run at one goal and draw the goalkeeper to that goal, but then change his mind and bend his run to attack and shoot at the other goal
- The shooter retrieves his ball and the goalkeeper returns to the flag to prepare for the next shooter
- The goalkeeper will need to be rotated every minute

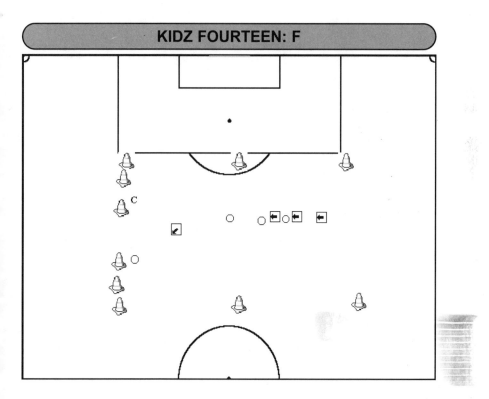

Pitch Size: 30yd x 30yd
No of players: Squad
Bibs: None
No of balls: 1 per player plus spares
No of markers: 10
Recommended Duration: 4 minutes

- The Coach, C, now makes two small goals
- The Coach (or one of the players) is the goalkeeper and this time he is able to move and is not restricted in any way
- The player must try to score in one of the goals

- As soon as a shot is taken, the next attacking player begins his run and players should be encouraged to take advantage of a goalkeeper who is out of position, or only covering one goal
- The goalkeeper will need to be rotated every minute

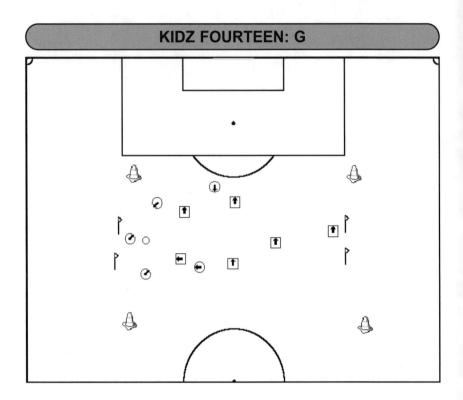

Pitch Size: 30yd x 30yd
No of players; Squad
Bibs: One or Two Sets
No of balls: 1 plus spares
No of markers: 4 plus 4 poles
Recommended Duration; 15 minutes

- Free play
- Five Reds play Five Blues in a normal game with minimal coaching, but lots of encouragement and reinforcement of good habits!

KIDZ FIFTEEN: A

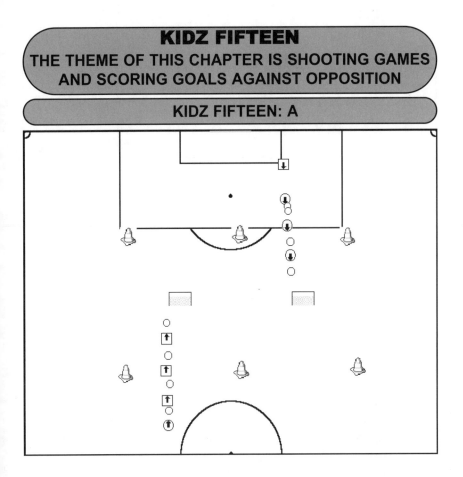

Pitch Size: 30yd x 30yd
No of players: Squad
Bibs: None
No of balls: 1 per player plus spares
No of markers: 8 plus 2 small goals
Recommended Duration: 5 minutes

- Players warm up for session by running their ball towards the first goal, scoring, and then moving onto the next goal to do the same

117

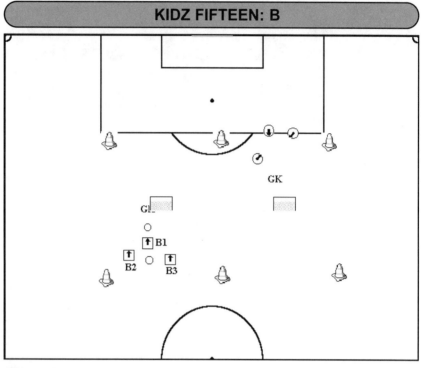

Pitch Size: 30yd x 30yd
No of players: Squad
Bibs: None
No of balls: 2 plus spares
No of markers: 6 plus 2 small goals
Recommended Duration: 8 minutes

- Coach splits squad into 2 in order to have two small sided games
- One player in each group is a goalkeeper
- The other players play against each other in a 1 v 1 v 1 competition, eg if B1 has the ball he is playing against both B2 and B3
- Each player has to try to score as many goals as he can
- Goals can be scored from either side of the goal (so try not to use a goal with a net)

- The Goalkeeper is rotated every two minutes

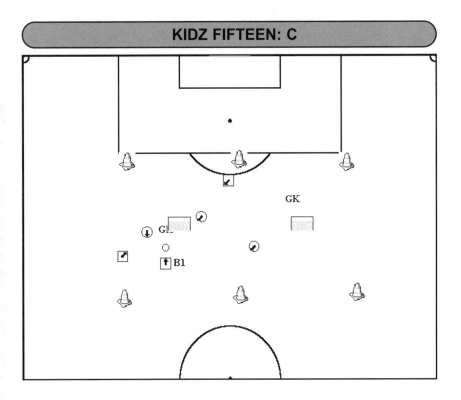

Pitch Size: 30yd x 30yd
No of players: Squad
Bibs: One or two sets
No of balls: 1 plus spares
No of markers: 6 plus 2 small goals
Recommended Duration: 8 minutes

- Coach splits squad into two teams with a goalkeeper each
- The goalkeeper plays with neither team, he only has to try to save each shot
- The Blues play the Reds across the whole pitch. The teams can score in either goal

- Goals can be scored from either side of the goal (so try not to use a goal with a net)
- The goalkeepers are rotated every two minutes

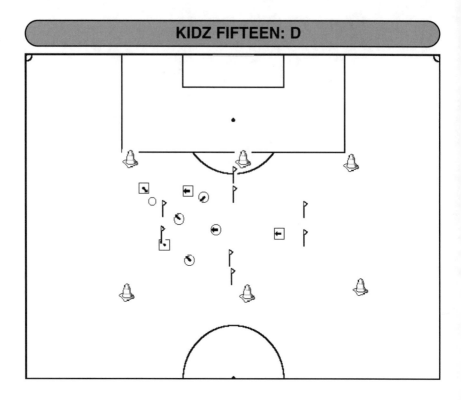

Pitch Size: 30yd x 30yd
No of players: Squad
Bibs: One or two sets
No of balls: 1 plus spares
No of markers: 6 plus 8 poles
Recommended Duration: 10 minutes

- Coach splits squad into two teams
- The Coach then places two goals (made with poles) on the half way line as in the diagram
- The Coach puts another two goals infield by 10yds from the center of the goal line as per the diagram

- No goalkeepers are used in this game so all players are outfield players and goals can only be prevented by tackling and intercepting the ball. The ball cannot be handled.
- Goals can be scored in any goal and from either side

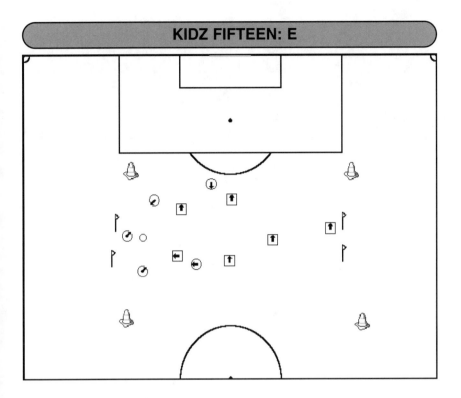

Pitch Size: 30yd x 30yd
No of players; Squad
Bibs: One or Two Sets
No of balls: 1 plus spares
No of markers: 4 plus 4 poles
Recommended Duration; 15 minutes

- Free play
- Five Reds play Five Blues in a normal game with minimal coaching, but lots of encouragement and reinforcement of good habits!

KIDZ SIXTEEN: A

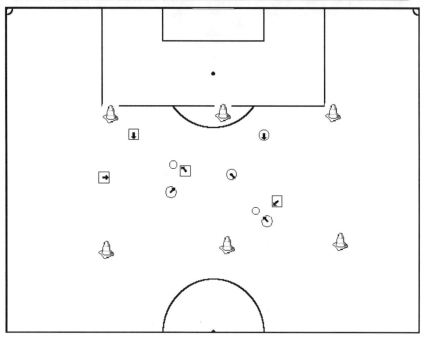

Pitch Size: 30yd x 30yd
No of players; Squad
Bibs: None
No of balls: 2 plus spares
No of markers: 6
Recommended Duration; 4 minutes

- Coach splits squad into two teams
- He takes one player from each team and places that player in the other grid. This player now becomes the defender
- The players now play 3 v 1 and try to keep the ball away from the defender
- Rotate the defender every minute

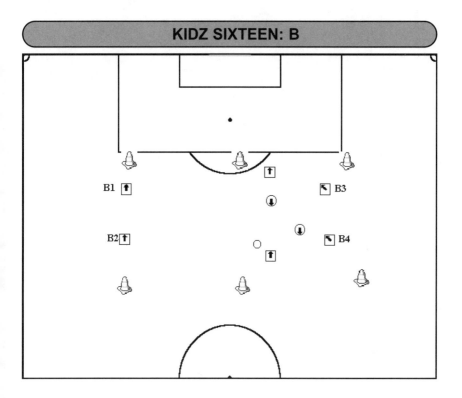

Pitch Size: 30yd x 30yd
No of players: Squad
Bibs: 2
No of balls: 1 plus spares
No of markers: 6
Recommended Duration: 8 minutes

- Coach splits squad into 6 Blues and 2 Reds
- The grid is split into two halves
- B1, B2, B3 and B4 must stay in their half of the grid
- The other two Blues are free to move from grid to grid
- The Blue players try to keep possession and stop the Reds from winning the ball
- The Reds gain a point each time they win possession
- The ball is then given back to the Blues and the players start again
- Rotate the defenders every two minutes

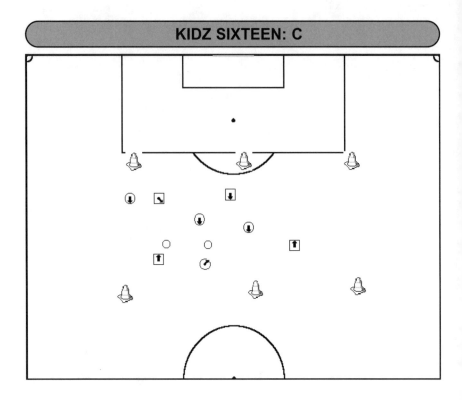

Pitch Size: 30yd x 30yd
No of players: Squad
Bibs: One or two sets
No of balls: 2 plus spares
No of markers: 6
Recommended Duration: 5 minutes

- Coach splits squad into Blues and Reds
- The Blues attempt to keep possession of their ball
- The Reds attempt to keep possession of their ball
- At the same time the Blues try to steal the Reds' ball and keep two balls, and the Reds do likewise

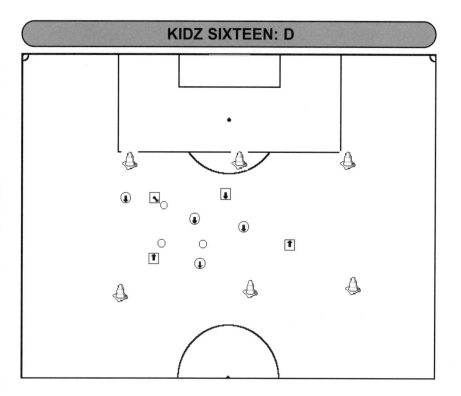

Pitch Size: 30yd x 30yd
No of players: Squad
Bibs: One or two sets
No of balls: 3 plus spares
No of markers: 6
Recommended Duration: 5 minutes

- Coach splits squad into Blues and Reds
- The Blues attempt to keep possession of their ball
- The Reds attempt to keep possession of their ball
- A third ball is also introduced into the game and this belongs to whichever team has the ball

- The aim of both teams is to try to gain possession of all three balls, and this is not easy!

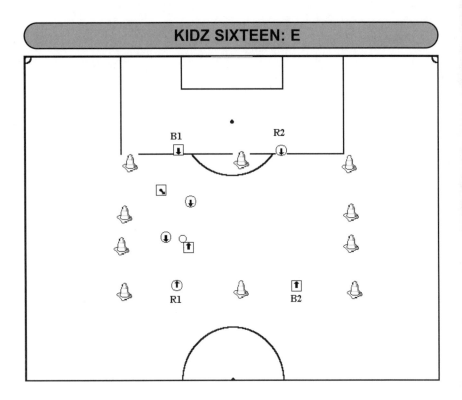

Pitch Size: 30yd x 30yd
No of players: Squad
Bibs: One or two sets
No of balls: 1 plus spares
No of markers: 10
Recommended Duration: 10 minutes

- Coach splits squad into Blues and Reds
- B1, B2, R1, and R2 are placed outside the grid as in the diagram
- The other Blues and Reds attempt to release B1, B2, or R1 and R2 so that they can join them and help them to win the game
- Players are released by simply playing the ball sucessfully to the player

- Once a team has released its two players that team can then try to score a goal in the normal fashion
- The Blues defend the Blue goal and attack the Red goal
- The Reds defend the Red goal and attack the Blue goal

- A team cannot score a goal until both of its players have been released

The winner is the first team to score three goals

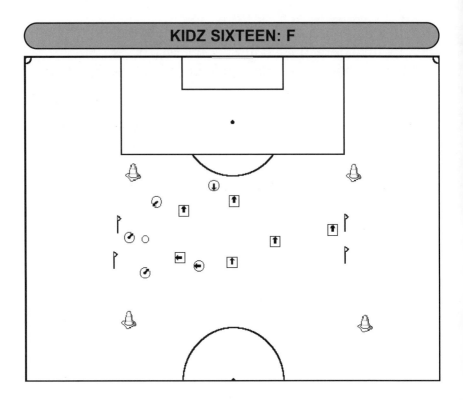

Pitch Size: 30yd x 30yd
No of players: Squad
Bibs: One or Two Sets
No of balls: 1 plus spares
No of markers: 4 plus 4 poles
Recommended Duration: 15 minutes

- Free play
- Five Reds play Five Blues in a normal game with minimal coaching, but lots of encouragement and reinforcement of good habits!

KIDZ SEVENTEEN
THE THEME OF THIS CHAPTER IS THE DEVELOPMENT OF COORDINATION AND AGILITY

KIDZ SEVENTEEN: A

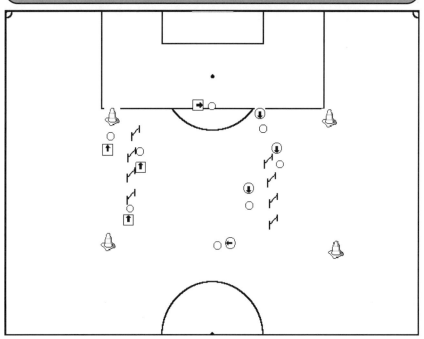

Pitch Size: 30yd x 30yd
No of players: Squad
Bibs: None
No of balls: 1 per player plus spares
No of markers: 4
No of Mini Hurdles 8 - 10
Recommended Duration: 5 minutes

- Players warm up by dribbling their ball through the Mini Hurdles as in the diagram

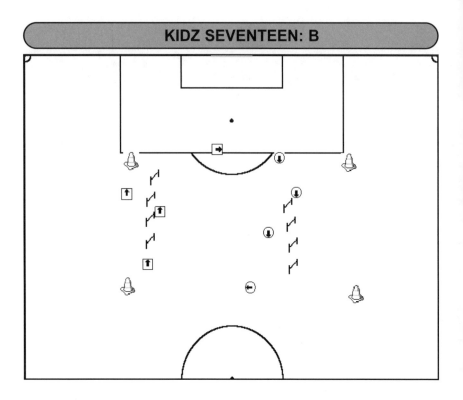

Pitch Size: 30yd x 30yd
No of players: Squad
Bibs: None
No of balls: 0
No of markers: 4
No of Mini Hurdles 8 - 10
Recommended Duration: 9 minutes

- Players run through the hurdles concentrating on making good sharp turns as they weave in and out of the obstacles
- The Coach should ensure that when the player has been weaving left to right, the player then plants his right foot hard into the ground before making the change to run right to left

- The Coach should either demonstrate this sharp turn himself and/or use one of the players as a demo player
- Again insist on good technique and good style
- 3 minutes

- Again the players weave through the hurdles by skipping side to side, leading with their right foot when they travel left to right and leading with their left foot when they travel right to left
- 3 minutes

- This time the players skip as they weave through the hurdles
- 3 minutes

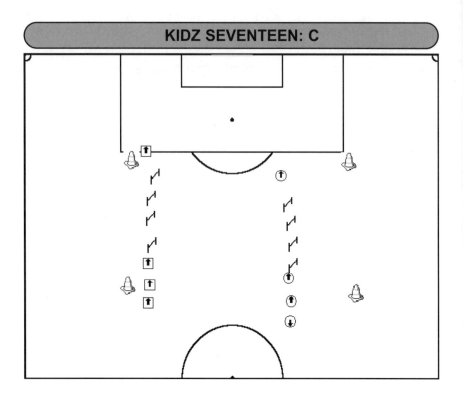

Pitch Size: 30yd x 30yd
No of players: Squad
Bibs: None
No of balls: 0
No of markers: 4
No of Mini Hurdles 8 - 10
Recommended Duration: 5 minutes

- Players race each other through the hurdles
- The second player in each file only begins his run once the first player has sprinted all the way back

- The Coach will notice that very often the better athletes have a superior running style to their teammates
- The Coach should highlight why they run better and try to get the other players to copy their style

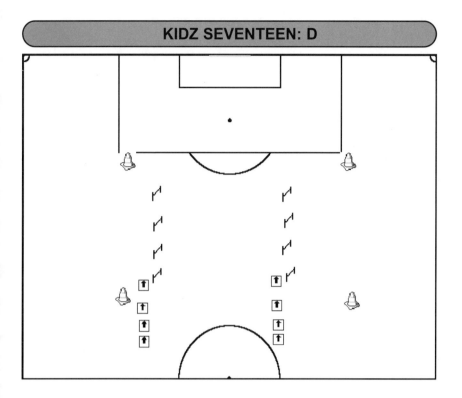

KIDZ SEVENTEEN: D

Pitch Size: 30yd x 30yd
No of players: Squad
Bibs: None
No of balls: 0
No of markers: 4
No of Mini Hurdles 8 - 10
Recommended Duration: 4 minutes

- Players line up so the their right foot is level with the out-side of the hurdle
- They then run at speed (or even race), but each time they come to another hurdle they have to lift their right foot off the ground to go over the hurdle
- 2 minutes
- The players then do the same as above, but this time with their left foot having to "jump" the hurdle
- 2 minutes

133

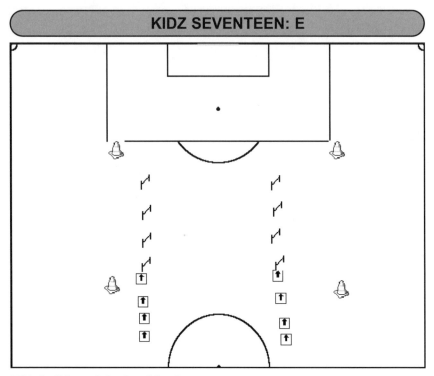

Pitch Size: 30yd x 30yd
No of players: Squad
Bibs: None
No of balls: 0
No of markers: 4
No of Mini Hurdles 8 - 10
Recommended Duration: 6 minutes

- Players line up central to the hurdles
- They race each other hopping on their left foot only
- Do this twice or perhaps three times and then switch to right foot only

- Players line up central to the hurdles again and this time with feet together they race each other by bounding through the hurdles with two footed jumps
- Two races only as too much of this type of plyometrics can be very exhausting

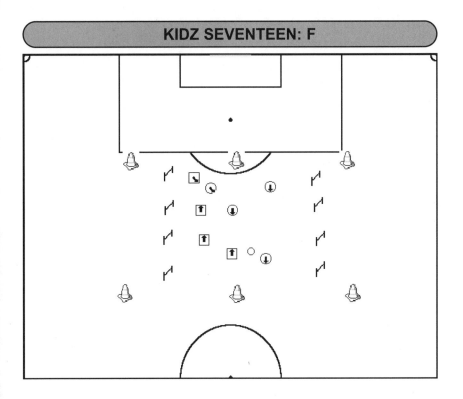

Pitch Size: 30yd x 30yd
No of players: Squad
Bibs: One or two sets
No of balls: 1 plus spares
No of markers: 6
No of Mini Hurdles 8 - 10
Recommended Duration: 10 minutes

- Players are divided into two teams
- The Blues have to defend their own hurdles and try to knock over the Reds' hurdles by kicking the ball against them
- The Reds do likewise

- The winners are the first team to knock over all of their opponent's hurdles

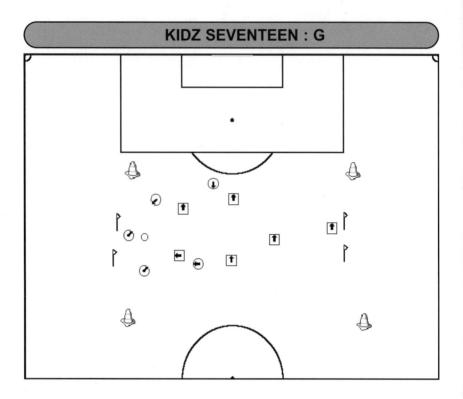

Pitch Size: 30yd x 30yd
No of players: Squad
Bibs: One or Two Sets
No of balls: 1 plus spares
No of markers: 4 plus 4 poles
Recommended Duration: 15 minutes

- Free play
- Five Reds play Five Blues in a normal game with minimal coaching, but lots of encouragement and reinforcement of good habits!

KIDZ EIGHTEEN: A

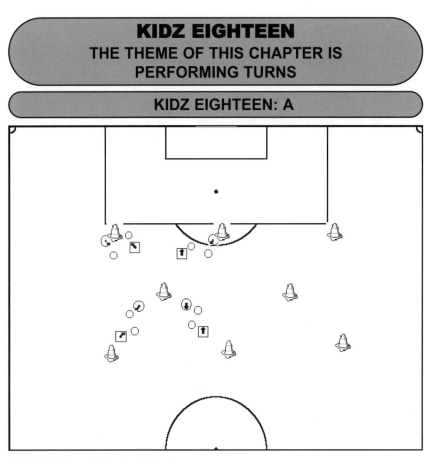

Pitch Size: 30yd x 30yd
No of players; Squad
Bibs: None
No of balls: 1 per player plus spares
No of markers: 8
Recommended Duration; 25 minutes

- Coach places two players on each corner marker
- The first player runs to the middle marker, turns, returns to the original marker and then player number two makes the same run
- The players can turn any way they like in this warm up
- 1 minute

- Players now run on their right foot only and turn on the inside of that foot
- This turn is called "The Inside Hook."
- 2 minutes

- As above, this time using the left foot
- 2 minutes

- Players now run on their right foot only and turn on the outside of that foot
- This turn is called "The Outside Hook."
- 2 minutes

- As above, this time using the left foot
- 2 minutes

- Players now run with the ball on their right foot to the marker
- At the marker they stop the ball with the sole of their right foot
- They then drag the ball behind them, turn and return home
- Player two now performs the same action
- This turn is called "The Drag Back."

- 2 minutes

- As above, this time using the left foot
- 2 minutes

- Players now run with the ball on their right foot
- Just before the player reaches the marker, he/she stops the ball and then takes another step forward so that all of his body is ahead of the ball
- The player then turns around and returns home with the ball
- This turn is called "The Stop Turn."
- 2 minutes

- As above, this time using the left foot
- 2 minutes

- Players now run with the ball on their right foot
- Just before they reach the marker the player steps over the ball with his right foot
- The player plants his foot firmly on the ground in front of his left foot
- They then pivot around on that right foot and end up facing the home marker
- The player now returns home running with the ball on his left foot
- This turn is called "The Step Over Turn."
- 2 minutes

- As above, this time using the left foot
- 2 minutes

- Players now run with the ball on their right foot
- Just before reaching the marker, the player moves the instep of his right foot over the ball and either slows the ball down or stops it
- The left foot is planted on the ground
- With his right foot, the player now knocks the ball behind him, turns and returns home
- This turn is called "The Cruyff Turn." after the legendary Dutch player and Coach Johan Cruyff

- 2 minutes

- As above, this time using the left foot
- 2 minutes

NOTE: THE COACH MUST DECIDE IF 25 MINUTES OF TURNING IS TOO MUCH FOR HIS PLAYERS. SOME PLAYERS ENJOY THIS LENGTH OF REPETITION WHEN THEY CAN SEE THEIR SKILLS IMPROVING. OTHERS MAY PREFER TO MIX UP THE TURNING DRILLS WITH GAMES. SOME MAY PREFER 1 MINUTE PER TURN, WHILE SOME MAY PREFER TO EXECUTE THREE TURNS IN ONE SESSION AND THREE IN ANOTHER.

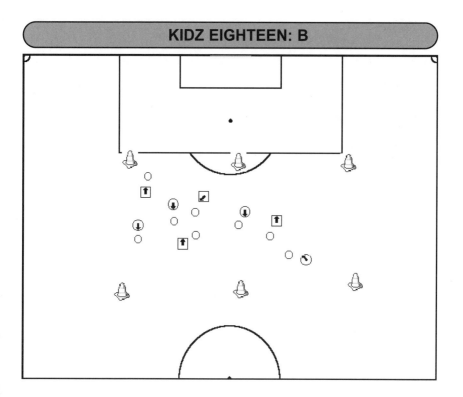

Pitch Size: 30yd x 30yd
No of players: Squad
Bibs: None
No of balls: 1 per player plus spares
No of markers: 6
Recommended Duration: 8 minutes

- VIRUS!
- The Coach tells his players that all of his teammates have a deadly VIRUS
- Each player has to run around the grid with their ball ensuring that he is at least a yard away from his infected colleagues!
- The Coach encourages the players to use all of the turns they learned at the beginning of this chapter to avoid certain death!

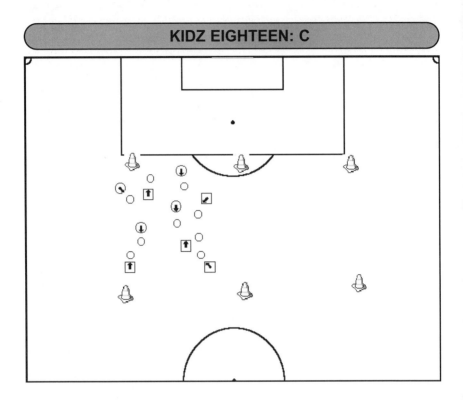

Pitch Size: 15yd x 15yd
No of players: Squad
Bibs: None
No of balls: 1 per player plus spares
No of markers: 4
Recommended Duration: 8 minutes

- VIRUS!
- The Coach tells his players that all of his teammates have a deadly VIRUS
- Each player has to run around the grid with a ball ensuring that he is at least a yard away from his infected colleagues!
- Unlike the last drill, the players have only half a field to work in and thus the drill becomes much harder!
- The Coach encourages the players to use all of the turns they learned at the beginning of this chapter to avoid certain death!

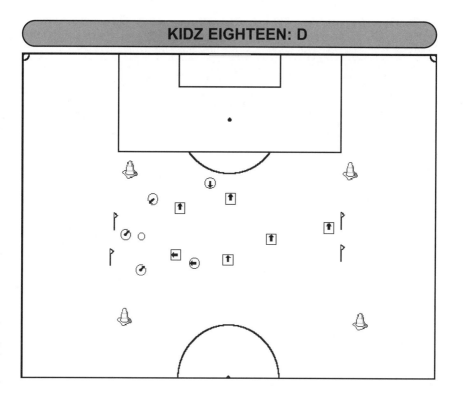

Pitch Size: 30yd x 30yd
No of players: Squad
Bibs: One or Two Sets
No of balls: 1 plus spares
No of markers: 8
Recommended Duration: 15 minutes

- Free play
- Five Reds play Five Blues in a normal game with minimal coaching, but lots of encouragement and reinforcement of good habits!

KIDZ NINETEEN
THE THEME OF THIS CHAPTER IS SCORING GOALS IN SHOOTING GAMES AND DRILLS

KIDZ NINETEEN: A

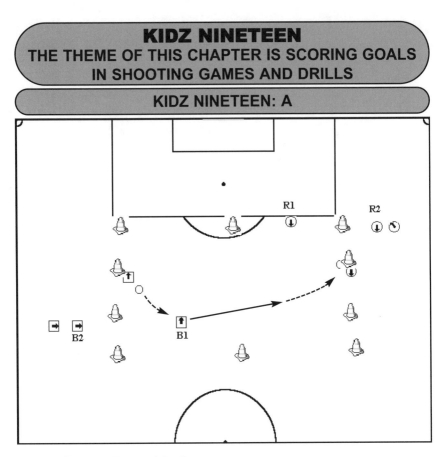

Pitch Size: 30yd x 30yd
No of players; Squad
Bibs: None
No of balls: 2 plus spares
No of markers: 10
Recommended Duration; 6 minutes

- In this warm up the Blue Goalkeeper throws the ball out to B1 who advances up the field passing the ball to the Red Goalkeeper at the top of the grid
- The Red Goalkeeper and R1 do likewise
- The Red Goalkeeper picks the ball up and throws it to his right to the next player in line, R2 etc.
- Rotate the Goalkeepers every minute
- After 3 minutes, goalkeepers throw to their left

144

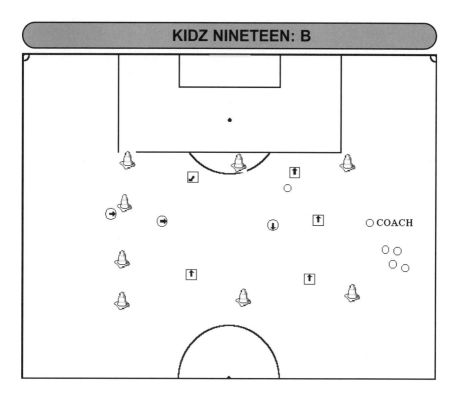

Pitch Size: 30yd x 30yd
No of players: Squad
Bibs: One or two sets
No of balls: 1 plus spares
No of markers: 10
Recommended Duration: 10 minutes

- The Coach divides the field into 2 equal 15yd x 15yd Zones
- The Coach acts as a server
- In the Zone nearest to the Coach the 3 Blue attackers attempt to keep the ball from the 1 Red defender
- Whenever they can the Blue attackers pass the ball to the 2 Blue strikers in the second Zone

- In the second Zone the Blues are faced with one defender and one goalkeeper
- The aim of the 2 Blue strikers is to score as many goals as possible

- The Coach should ensure that the Blue players in both Zones spread out as much as possible and make it difficult for the Reds to defend
- Players should be encouraged to play the ball to the two strikers as often as possible BUT only when this is possible. The Coach should try to teach his players patience as opposed to blindly kicking the ball forward

- The Blue strikers should be encouraged to shoot when they can, and when they are being marked, they should be encouraged to pass to their partner

- Goalkeepers and Defenders are rotated every two minutes

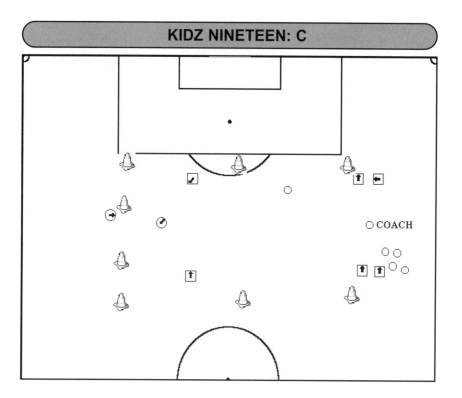

Pitch Size: 30yd x 30yd
No of players: Squad
Bibs: None
No of balls: 6 - 8
No of markers: 10
Recommended Duration: 5 minutes

- The Coach puts one player in goal with one defender in front of him
- The remaining players attack the goal in pairs and try to score by dribbling past the defender, drawing the defender and then passing to their team mate, playing wall passes, long range shooting etc etc

- Defenders and Goalkeepers are rotated every minute

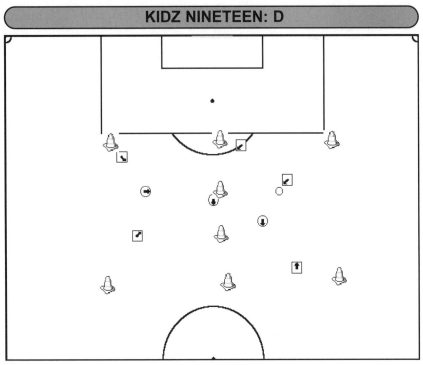

Pitch Size: 30yd x 30yd
No of players: Squad
Bibs: One or two sets
No of balls: 1 plus spares
No of markers: 10
Recommended Duration: 10 minutes

- The Coach places a goal in the middle of the grid
- 1 Goalkeeper and 2 Red defenders are faced by 5 Blue attacking players
- The Blues aim to score as many goals as they can
- They can score from either side of the goal
- The Coach should encourage the attacking players to spread out
- They should also be encouraged to have players in both halves of the field
- The Coach should show the players how to switch the ball from one zone to the other as an effective attacking ploy
- Goalkeepers and Defenders are rotated every two minutes

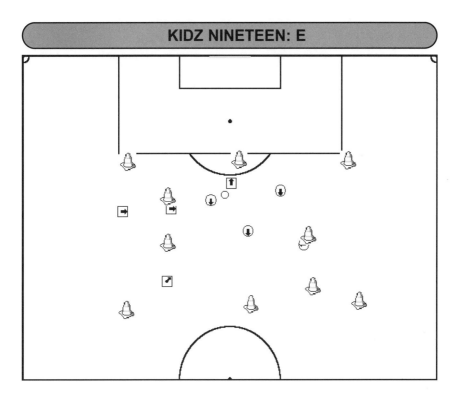

Pitch Size: 30yd x 30yd
No of players: Squad
Bibs: One or two sets
No of balls: 1 plus spares
No of markers: 10
Recommended Duration: 10 minutes

- The Coach places two goals in the middle of the grid
- This time we have two equal teams with one goalkeeper for each team
- The object of both teams is to score as many goals past either goalkeeper

- Goalkeepers are rotated every two minutes

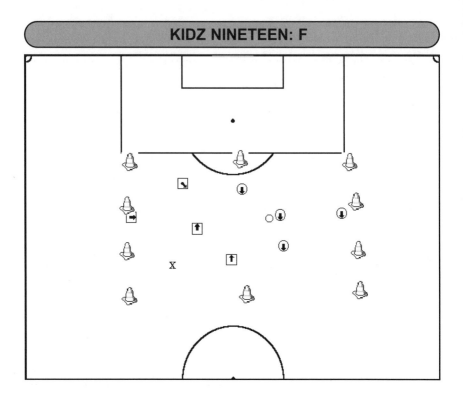

Pitch Size: 30yd x 30yd
No of players: Squad
Bibs: One or two sets
No of balls: 1 plus spares
No of markers: 10
Recommended Duration: 10 minutes

- The Coach splits the squad into two teams
- The Coach or an additional player, X, plays with the team in possession

- Both teams try to score as many goals as possible

- Goalkeepers are rotated every two minutes

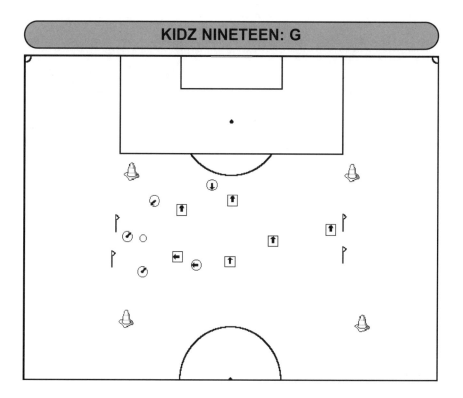

Pitch Size: 30yd x 30yd
No of players: Squad
Bibs: One or Two Sets
No of balls: 1 plus spares
No of markers: 4 plus 4 poles
Recommended Duration: 15 minutes

- Free play
- Five Reds play Five Blues in a normal game with minimal coaching, but lots of encouragement and reinforcement of good habits!

KIDZ TWENTY

THE THEME OF THIS CHAPTER IS
FUN AND GAMES AND BOREDOM BREAKERS
(FOR CERTAIN TIMES IN THE SEASON!)

KIDZ TWENTY: A

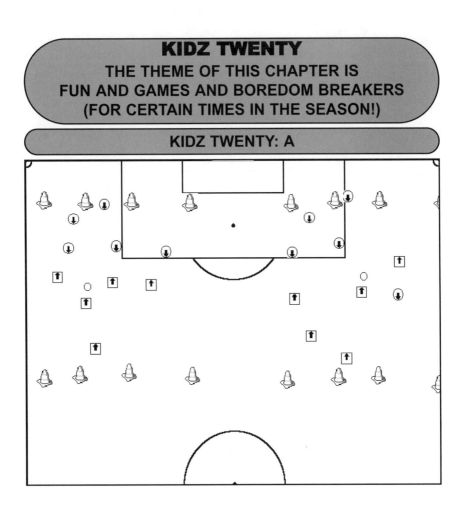

Pitch size: Half field
Number of players: 4 Teams
Number of balls: 2 plus spares
Bibs: 2 or 4 sets
Number of Markers: 16 or 8 small goals
Recommended Duration: Whole Training Session

- MINI WORLD CUP
- The Coach gets together with three other teams and books a half field for a training night
- After a brief warm up, each team plays each other in a game for a pre-determined time

- If the Coach has 1 hour for his training the times may look like this....

0 - 10 minutes Team 1 v Team 2 : Team 3 v Team 4
10 - 20 minutes Team 1 v Team 3 : Team 2 v Team 4
20 - 30 minutes Team 1 v Team 4 : Team 2 v Team 3

At the end of this 30 minute period we now have a league table with a 1st, 2nd, 3rd and 4th placed team. Now we can have grand finals!

30 minutes - 45 minutesSemi Final 1 : 1st Team v 4thTeam
                       Semi Final 2 : 2nd Team v
3rdTeam

45 minutes - 60 minutes Grand Final (Winners of the two
                        Semis play each other)
                        Third Place play off (Losers of the
                        two Semis play each other)

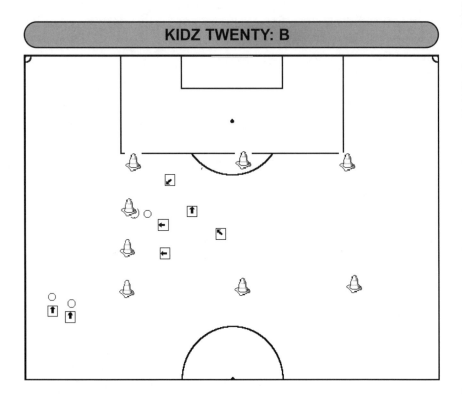

Pitch size: Half field
Number of players: Squad
Number of balls: 1 plus spares
Bibs: None
Number of Markers: 8
Recommended Duration: 30 minutes

- WEMBLEY/CUP FINALS
- This game has been played in English schoolyards for decades!

- The Coach puts out the pitch and places one member of the squad in goal
- The Goalkeeper throws the ball out into general play to no one in particular

- The outfield players are on their own and when they get the ball they have to try to score knowing that they face every other member of the squad!

- If a player scores he comes out of the game because he has progressed to the next round
- This player may juggle a ball on the sideline while waiting for the next round

- One player is eliminated in each round and this is the player who fails to score

- Eventually we get to a Finals situation where there are only two players left in the game
- Usually in the Final it is the first player to score 2 or 3 goals that wins

- This can be a great game BUT the Coach should be aware that at any time there are likely to be a number of players not actively involved in the activity. Unless they are watching and enjoying the tournament (which can be very good for team bonding!) the Coach may have to organize something formally for these players

- It may be good to play WEMBLEY when the players have had a lot of soccer and traditional training and they are looking for a rest or something different

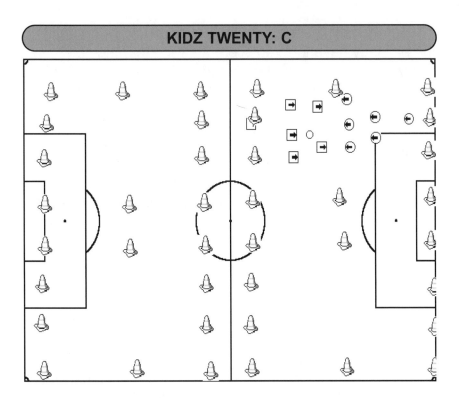

Pitch size: Full field
Number of players: Lots!
Number of balls: 1 per game plus spares
Bibs: 1 or 2 per game. Uniforms may be worn
Number of Markers: 8 per game, or 0 if Junior fields plus goals are used
Recommended Duration: Half to Full Day

- CARNIVAL!
- Many Clubs organize a day when all of the teams in a particular age group are able to compete against against each other in a Carnival
- Usually outside teams are also invited, but it could be that there are more than enough internal teams to successfully run a Carnival

- For many parents and players who have never experienced true competition, since points are very often not awarded in junior soccer, Carnivals can be a very exciting time! The coach's mathematical ability is also challenged... "If we win 2:0 and they lose 6:1 we could get to the Semis unless the other team wins 5:0 and....!"

- Probably the ideal time would be games lasting 20 minutes (Two 10 minute halves) with only the briefest half time for a very quick drink and a few instructions from the Coach
- The players have at least 20 or 40 minutes rest between the games

- The Carnivals my teams have entered have usually involved 10 to 12 teams split into two groups
- This guarantees 4 or 5 group games on the day, regardless of the team progressing to the Finals
- The winners of the two groups play the second placed teams in the other group in the Semis
- The winners of the two Semis progress onto the Final
- The Semis and Final are often of a slightly longer duration, perhaps 15 minute halves. Administrators have to be aware however that this may be very tiring for the young players
- Although they can be a lot of work, Carnivals can be a lot of fun!
- The Club usually makes a lot of money from sales of food and drink, and a well run competition does a lot to promote the organization
- The Coach has a hard job in the sense that the players need to rest between games and eat and drink sensibly. This can prove to be quite a challenge given the many distractions and atmosphere of the day!
- The Coach may also find that the parents become more intense than they have in the past because there are ribbons and trophies at stake!

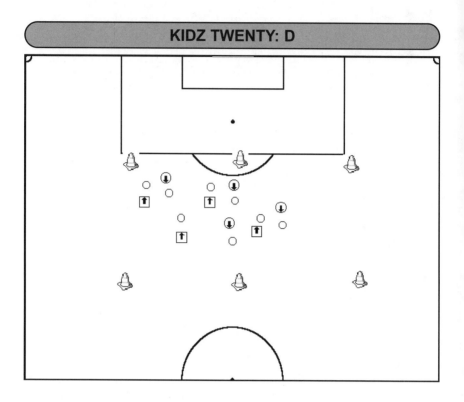

Pitch size: 30yd x 30yd
Number of players: Squad
Number of balls: 1 per player plus spares
Bibs: None
Number of Markers: 8
Recommended Duration: 20 minutes

- Each player has a ball and after a brief warm up the coach begins the ball juggling competition
- Players try to be the champion of juggling using...

> any body part feet: head, chest etc
> right foot only
> left foot only
> juggling off the thighs
> keeping the ball up performing headers
> juggling the ball while traveling 20 yards (walking or jogging)

- Very young players will definitely have difficulties with some of the juggling. Even most 9 year olds will struggle a little with some of the more difficult ball control excercises
- If they can see the Coach or a more skilled older player perform such tricks, however, it gives them something long term to aim for, and a skill they can aquire by practicing themselves in their back yard

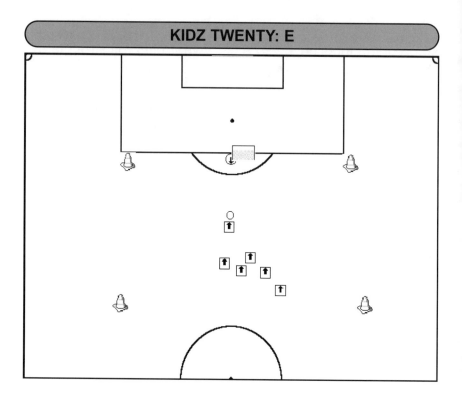

Pitch size: 30yd x 30yd
Number of players: Squad
Number of balls: 1 per player plus spares
Bibs: None
Number of Markers: 4 plus a small goal
Recommended Duration: 10 minutes

- PENALTIES!
- The Coach puts one of the squad in goal
- All of the other players then line up to take Penalties

- If they score they progress to the next round
- If they miss they drop out

- The Winner is the player who stays in the game the longest and scores the most goals

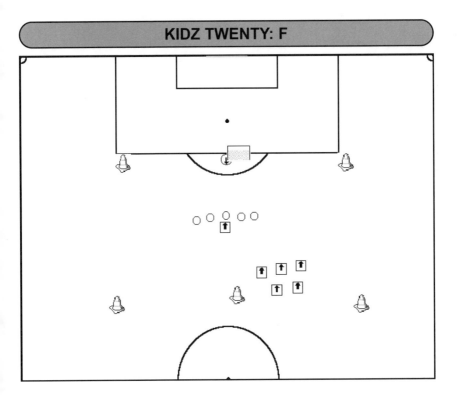

Pitch size: 30yd x 30yd
Number of players: Squad
Number of balls: 5
Bibs: None
Number of Markers: 4 plus a small goal
Recommended Duration: 10 minutes

- The Coach places 5 balls in a line in front of the goal
- Players have to run from the marker and shoot at goal
- They then run back to the marker, turn, run and shoot the second ball at goal
- The Coach must encourage the players to use both their right and left feet to shoot (balls on left side of player use left foot : balls on right side of player use right foot)
- This continues until they have had 5 shots
- The winner is the player who scores the most goals

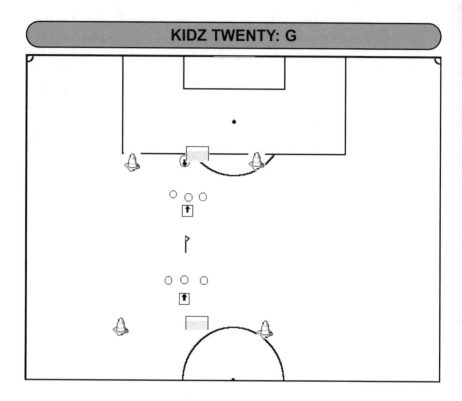

Pitch size: 10yd x 40yd
Number of players: Squad
Number of balls: 6
Bibs: None
Number of Markers: 4 plus 2 small goals and 1 pole
Recommended Duration: 10 minutes

- The Coach places 3 balls in front of each goal
- Players have to run from the marker and shoot at the first goal
- They then run to the next set of balls and shoot at the second goal
- The Coach must encourage the players to use both their right and left feet to shoot (balls on left side of player use left foot : balls on right side of player use right foot)
- This continues until they have had 6 shots
- The winner is the player who scores the most goals

KIDZ TWENTY ONE
A SAMPLE PRACTICE SESSION

The following is a sample practice session made up of several drills and games from the book. This is just one of the limitless combinations you can use!

KIDZ SEVEN: A

KIDZ EIGHT: B

KIDZ TEN: C

KIDZ ELEVEN: C

KIDZ NINETEEN: D

KIDZ NINETEEN: B

FINISH WITH A FREE GAME OF 5V5

CHAPTER TWENTY TWO
USING A SCHEDULE TO ROTATE JUNIOR TEAMS

Most Soccer Federations around the world would advocate equal time on the field for all young players. That there are Coaches in charge of six-year-olds who keep their weakest players on the bench for much of the time is obscene, but it does happen!

The training in this book has been geared towards players of six, seven and eight years of age. At this level the players should all receive equal playing time. No matter how frustrated the coach may get with a weaker player, a player who does not seem to be learning about the game, is letting his teammates down, or who is only there because his parents have forced him to be there. Perhaps the only reason a player should not get equal time on the field is when that player is consistently missing training. Players have to learn the importance of training from an early age and if there is a persistent offender it could be that he deserve less playing time. This does however depend very much upon club policy. A compassionate Coach may realize that the absences have nothing to do with the child. It could be the parent's situation which makes it difficult for the player to attend training. The Coach may therefore find it difficult at times to apply rules which are too rigid, even though older players will almost certainly find themselves bound by such rules.

It is important that the Coach makes as many things as possible predictable and orderly when he is in a position to manage a situation. This can considerably reduce tension and lead to better performances in training and games.

The purpose of this book is to give the Coach complete training sessions that he can use for the whole of his one-hour or allotted training time. The organization and design of the training session, the necessary resources, the splitting up of the players, etc have already been prepared.

On Game Day the Coach, the players and their parents can also be more organized with the use of an effective roster such as the one shown in Diagram One.

Why bother?

The schedule does a number of things:
- It first of all shows the parents and the players when they will be playing, when they will be on the bench and, in this case, when it will be their week off. It is not imperative that players are given a week off every so often , but with the number of players I was working with in 2001 both myself and the parents thought that the situation would be easier to manage with one player rested every nine games
- Everyone is aware of when it is his turn to be in goal. Some parents like to stand by the side of the goal when their child is the goalkeeper to help keep them focused and to assist with this difficult job
- It shows the parents that everyone has exactly the same time on the field and on the bench. They can (and will!) check your figures and if you have made a mistake, I am sure you will amend the schedule
- The timing of the substitutions is written down and the Coach does not have to think who should come off and who should stay on. This may seem crazy if you are in a very tight game and you have to take off your best player, but as you will see the schedule is designed so that substitutions have the least damaging effect on the strength of the team. As we said before on this point, players and coaches at this level should not be overly concerned with winning. It's all about development, and that is why many federations do not even keep results and draw up league tables for young players
- And now to contradict myself, a wily Coach can actually use the schedule to ensure that he is fielding the best team when that game with the arch rival rolls around!

Diagram One.. A Roster for a Junior Team

1 - ALI		6 - ROBIN	
2 - EARL		7 - BRIAN	
3 - NORMAN		8 - MICHAEL	
4 - ASTRO		9 - BUNNY	
5 - JAMES			

- I had nine players to work with in 2001 and I drew up a grid like the one above
- Games were played with one goalkeeper and five outfield players
- Players 1, 4 and 7 were the best players in the squad at that time, players 2, 5 and 8 the next best and players 3, 6 and 9 the next best
- During the season the players improved and I could have moved the group around to reflect their changed status. Some Coaches may choose to reconsider the order of the players half way through the season if they want to. I did not simply because I knew that when I was supposedly playing some of my weaker players in fact they were as good as or almost as good as some of the so called better players. I couldn't loose!
- In my experience, however, during these early years if the players are not graded there will usually be between 1 - 3 players who are not up to the same standard of the stronger athletes
- As you can see from the rotations below, it was very rare for players 1, 4 and 7 to be on the field at the same time. Similarly, you would not see all the best players on the pitch and the least able on the bench. Why? Simply because if you make substitutions and take two good players off and replace them with two lesser players the impact on the team can be quite dramatic. While results are not important at this level, you still want the players to play as well as they can and this can be helped by considering the balance of the team

- The schedule below therefore ensures that the players are mixed up in terms of their ability, and while you may not play your best side at any point, nor will you play your weakest.

- With only five outfield players on the field, I decided that three players on the bench was too many and suggested to the parents that each player have one week off in a nine week cycle to reduce the number of substitutes to a more manageable two

- Each player is rested one game in nine. In Week One below Bunny missed the first game

- Each player will have 12 ten minute periods on the bench per 9 game cycle

- The first named players on the Rosters are Goalkeepers. In Week One the goalkeeper was Ali for the whole of the first half

- The second named player is the Goalkeeper for the second half. In Week One this was Earl

- Goalkeepers play one full half, and then play the remaining half on the field without being substituted. In Week One Ali and Earl both played the whole game, but for half of it they were in goal

- A lucky Coach may have a player who wants to become a goal-keeper and who is good in goal. While this is great in many respects, I think that it is important that all players experience what it is like to play in goal at this early age. Similarly, the bud-ding Brad Freidel should get the chance to experience what it is like to play on the field

- The clever Coach will probably want to ensure that when his team does play a good team that the more skilful goalkeepers are between the posts

- Likewise, it could be arranged that one of the weaker players has his week off when the team plays a harder team

- The weaker player may also get his turn in goal against a team who will not be too daunting

- When the team plays a weaker team that is the time for giving players 3, 6 and 9 more time on the field. This may seem contra-dictory in the sense that I have argued the case for giving all players equal time (which they do get), and yet I am advocating a degree of selectivity in picking the side at times. I would stand by this since it happens rarely and a weaker player who is dominat-ed by a stronger opponent will not get much out of this experi-ence, whereas he may not be put off by having more time against opponents of a similar standard

- Any Coach who is going to stick to a schedule similar to the one here will find that he will not be able to "hide" the weaker players many times at all and therefore they will be exposed to stronger opposition on a reasonably regular basis
- "Hiding" may involve giving a player a complete game against a lesser team and perhaps half a game against a more difficult opponent. If you look at the schedule below I never actually did this in 2001, but the potential to amend the schedule is obviously there
- Substitutions are made one quarter through the allotted playing time strictly according to the schedule. For my Junior Team in 2001, who were faced with 20 minute halves, in Week One after ten minutes players 3 and 4 (Norman and Astro) came off, and players 7 and 8 (Brian and Michael) came on
- If parents know they are going to be out of town on a particular week they can ask the Coach for the roster to be changed. For example if Bunny knows he is going to be away in Week 2, but is down to miss Week 1, then the Coach can check to see if it is convenient for Michael to swap and miss Week 1 instead of Week 2.
- The Coach tries to be flexible with schedules like this, but I have certainly had occasions when it has not been possible to accommodate all of the changes that some people have wanted and it can be possible that some players may have to have two games off per cycle. A Coach who keeps good records may be able to amend this in the next cycle of games.

WEEK ONE

```
1 2 3 4 5 6   SUB 7 8
1 2 5 6 7 8        3 4
2 1 7 8 3 4        5 6
2 1 7 4 5 6        3 8
```

Player rested, number 9 Bunny

WEEK TWO
3 4 5 6 7 9 SUB 1 2
3 4 7 9 1 2   5 6
4 3 1 2 5 6   7 9
4 3 5 6 7 9   1 2
Player rested, number 8 Michael

WEEK THREE
5 6 3 1 2 8 SUB 9 4
5 6 1 8 3 4   9 2
6 5 3 4 9 1   2 8
6 5 9 1 2 8   3 4
Player rested, number 7 Brian

WEEK FOUR
7 8 2 3 4 5 SUB   1 9
7 8 4 5 1 9   2 3
8 7 1 9 2 3   4 5
8 7 2 3 4 5   1 9
Player rested, number 6 Robin

WEEK FIVE
9 1 2 3 4 6 SUB   8 7
9 1 4 6 8 7   2 3
1 9 8 7 2 3   4 6
1 9 2 3 4 6   8 7
Player rested, number 5 James

WEEK SIX
2 3 6 8 9 5 SUB 1 7
2 3 7 8 1 9   6 5
3 2 1 9 6 8   7 5
3 2 6 8 7 5   1 9
Player rested, number 4 Astro

WEEK SEVEN
4 5 7 1 9 2 SUB   6 8
4 5 9 2 6 8   7 1
5 4 6 8 7 1   9 2
5 4 7 1 9 2   6 8
Player rested, number 3 Norman

WEEK EIGHT

6 7 1 9 8 3   SUB 5 4
6 7 8 3 5 4   1 9
7 6 5 4 1 9   8 3
7 6 1 9 8 3   5 4
Player rested, number 2 Earl

WEEK NINE

8 9 3 5 4 2   SUB 7 6
8 9 4 2 7 6   3 5
9 8 7 6 3 5   4 2
9 8 7 5 4 2   3 6
Player rested, number 1 Ali

This schedule worked well for me in 2001 and it removed a lot of pressure when it came to deciding who should come off and when. It also ensured fairness in terms of time on the field, despite the fact that I might still on occasions choose my rotations to match the teams we were playing against.

The parents were also very pleased with knowing that their children had equal time, knowing when they would be substitutes, in goal, resting etc. Many of them looked forward to having a week off which is quite understandable given the demands of soccer on many parents' weekends.

I can imagine that some Coaches and parents may object to the idea that I have talked about arranging the schedule to "hide" the weaker players. I would repeat that…it cannot be done very often if you are truly committed to giving all of the player's equal time on the field. I only manipulated the schedule against two teams in particular (our strongest and weakest opponents), and even then it was only for one of the three times that we played each team.

A responsible Coach will not turn players off the game. In 2000 I had a player who was not especially good and I doubted that he would be back the next year. I was always wary about playing him against one particular team since they were both very good and very physical. I consequently limited his time on the field against this team (usually to half a game minimum), but made up his time in lesser games. In 2001 the player evolved into one of the best players in the squad and I had no hesitation in playing him in any game.

Again, I think a responsible Coach has to be receptive to his players and if they do appear timid or overwhelmed by certain opponents or teams, then it could be that the bench or a rest may be the best place for that player on that day. This is not to say that the same situation would not change the very next day! One final note on the idea of "hiding": even eight year olds are not stupid! While my own son is a good attacking field player, I don't think he will ever have clubs lining up to sign him as a goal-keeper. I consequently hid him (and other players in the team like him) and only played him in goal against the weaker teams. One night in the car going home from training he announced that he was tired of only being played in goal against the weaker teams. He wanted to face the strongest team that weekend between the posts. I tried to talk him out of it, but he had seen through my rotation!

Most parents are smarter than the average eight-year-old and they too will see through any obvious and persistent attempts to hide their child. The fact that you have not shown faith in their child can be demotivating in itself and may help to turn them off the game!

As always in a situation like this a wise Coach will communicate. Communicate with the player and with the parent. The Coach will tell them what he thinks and see what they think. Like we have said before, you are not playing for the World Cup Final or your own glory.

At the end of the day the best Coach at this level is probably not the one whose team wins 18:0 every week (but with the best team on the field all of the time). It is the Coach who has a group of players who ...

- **have fun**
- **learn about the game**
- **develop skills**

- learn how to lose and win
- learn about team play
- learn a little about being responsible
- learn a little about game preparation
- have more fun
- and are back next year

... If you can achieve the above, you have been a success!